BLACK FATHERS

BLACK FATHERS

◆

A CALL FOR HEALING

KRISTIN
CLARK TAYLOR

DOUBLEDAY

New York   London   Toronto
Sydney   Auckland

"My Father's Ways" by Lenard D. Moore from *Forever Home* by Lenard D. Moore, Saint Andrews Press, October 1992.

"Father's Pledge" by Haki R. Madhubuti from *Black Men: Obsolete, Single, Dangerous?* by Haki R. Madhubuti, Third World Press, 1990. Reprinted by permission of the author.

"New Beginnings" by Helen Steiner Rice from *Everyone Needs Someone.* Fleming Revell Co., 1987.

"Tickle Tickle" by Dakari Hru. From *In Daddy's Arms I Am Tall: African Americans Celebrating Fathers.* Text copyright © by Dakari Hru. Reprinted by arrangement with Lee and Low Books Inc., 95 Madison Avenue, New York, NY 10016

PUBLISHED BY DOUBLEDAY
a division of Random House, Inc.
1745 Broadway, New York, New York 10019

DOUBLEDAY and the portrayal of an anchor with a dolphin are trademarks of Doubleday, a division of Random House, Inc.

Book design by Jennifer Ann Daddio

Library of Congress Cataloging-in-Publication Data
Taylor, Kristin Clark.
Black fathers : a call for healing / Kristin Clark Taylor.—1st ed.
    p.   cm.
1. African American fathers.   2. Fatherhood—United States.
I. Title.

HQ756 .T39 2003
306.874'2'08996073—dc21
2002073872

ISBN 0-385-50249-4
Copyright © 2003 Kristin Clark Taylor

For my father, James W. Clark

ACKNOWLEDGMENTS

Imust begin by issuing a trilogy of thanks to three fathers whose grace and guidance have forever changed the course of my life and whose mere presence in the world justifies the reason for this book's existence.

Always, first and foremost, everlasting thanks and praise to my heavenly Father, my Lord and Savior Jesus Christ, who ordered my steps to His word and guided my hands as I wrote. It is through Him that all of my blessings flow. It is through Him that the rest of this miraculous trilogy is made manifest and perfect in its form. Through Him, I have been given the gift of the two other perfect components that make up this trilogy of thanks:

My earthly father, James W. Clark, is a vital part of this trilogy of gratitude. Sitting now at the right hand of Christ the King, what my father left for me is alive and living: his memory. The moments. The magic of his friendship. And now that he is gone, the gift of his spiritual presence. Thank you, Daddy, for your constant, protective gaze from heaven while I wrote this book. Thank you for guiding me back toward the cobwebbed memories of my childhood and helping me focus on things I thought I'd long since forgotten. Had it not been for your constant presence, how in the world could I have written this book? How would I have ever remembered, for instance, that the precise color of the crayon I selected to draw my first picture for you in nursery school was "Candy Apple Red" if it hadn't been for your gentle spirit that nudged me directly to the drawing itself, still neatly tucked away at the very bottom of my Forever Box? Thank you, Father, for propelling me forward in ways that sometimes even I don't understand. Every page of this book is steeped in your memory and spirit.

What completes this trilogy is the presence of yet a third father, a miracle of a man named Lonnie P. Taylor, the father of our two children and my best friend. What remains, again, are more questions than answers: How can I thank you for the miracle that *is* you? How is it possible to gauge the measure of a man whose depth of character knows no bounds? Why *is* it that my Heavenly Father is so good, so merciful, and so kind that He sent me you? Perhaps answers are not even in order here. Perhaps all I really need know is that you exist in the world. Perhaps a pure and simple "thank you"—for everything you do and everything you are—is all that needs to flow from my pen.

Gratitude and gratefulness, also, to my six older siblings, Joann Anderson, Noelle Clark, Donald Clark, Tanya Clark, Nikki Clark, and Ingrid Draper, for surrounding me with love and laughter as I wrote. Praise and thanks also to my angel here on earth, Mrs. Magdalene S. Taylor, and the entire Taylor family. I love you all.

Profound thanks to the miraculous women friends in my life whose spirits are somehow—in some certain, unique, and inextricable way— bound closely to mine: Paige Anderson, Phyllis Armstrong, Bryna Berman, Karen Gaddis, Nancy Kleinman, Laura Randolph Lancaster, Novellia Pounds, Julie Stoppel, Beatrice Welters, and Vickie West. You are my sisters, all. Thank you for not only offering me your collective shoulder to lean on, but for opening your hearts to me as I wrote.

This book could not have been born into the world without the urgent coaching of my editor and literary midwife, Janet Hill, who first identified a heartbeat in the form of a manuscript long before I even heard a murmur, and who never once left my side throughout the entire labor and delivery of this book. Never once. Janet: It was your brilliance that helped steer this manuscript toward the light of day. Your faith and friendship are a blessing in my life, beautiful in their simplicity and purity.

To my agent, Madeleine Morel, deepest gratitude to you for nudging me along and keeping my feet to the fire and my hands on the keyboard. You, too, believed in me before the beginning, before this project evolved from an abstraction to reality. Never once did your confidence and clarity waver.

The people at Doubleday are brimming with brilliance. I am blessed to have had such brilliance, enthusiasm, and creativity shower itself onto the pages of this book. To Stephen Rubin, president and publisher of Doubleday, Bill Thomas, editor in chief, and Michael Palgon, deputy publisher, profound thanks for believing in me yet again. Your collective energy and quiet support define what true leadership—particularly in the publishing world—is all about. Thanks, also, to Chava Boylan, Jennifer Ann Daddio, John Fontana, Rebecca Holland, Tracy Jacobs, Meredith McGinnis, and Laura Pillar. You are the special ones who help Doubleday shine. A special thanks, also, to Nora Reichard, for her patience and professionalism as we fine-tuned the copy. And finally, to the wise and wonderful Emma Bolton, the first face I see when I visit Doubleday's offices in New York, thank you for your shining spirit. During editing sessions, I'd keep the vision of your warm smile tucked away inside my spiritual pocket, and when the sessions got grim or tedious (and sometimes they *did*, I must admit!), I'd pull out your smile and carry on!

To the scores of people I interviewed for this book, my boundless thanks for sharing your stories, your strength, your smiles, and your souls. Your words alone speak for themselves. I pray that they will uplift and inspire many.

To my friend Jason Miccolo Johnson, who has provided much of the visual weight to this project by sharing some of his soul-searing photos:

thank you for pouring such powerful images onto the pages of this book. I admire you not only for your talent as a photographer (the best I know), but for your tenacity for putting up with the likes of me on yet another of our literary journeys together.

And finally, happily, a heartfelt thanks to my two children, the two living miracles who came into this world through me, Lonnie Paul and Mary Elizabeth Taylor: my mother-love for both of you knows no bounds. It is not of this world. It is from another place, somewhere deeper than I've ever been before or ever will go again. I've loved you both for far longer than I've known you—long before you ever even came into the world. I even loved the *idea* of you, and I counted the moments until we met. Thank you for your patience, and for backing quietly out of the room when you saw me writing or conducting an interview. Thank you, also, for being a vital part of this book by writing such beautiful, heartfelt pieces about your dad. Your writing makes me very, very proud. I love you both. You are the fire in my soul.

Peace and Blessings,
Kristin Clark Taylor

CONTENTS

CONTENTS

BLACK FATHERS

My Father's Ways

I.

You perched me on a stool
like a beach bird on a branch,
teach me my times tables
that multiply like rabbits.

II.

You take me to football games,
coach me, draw plays
in symbols
on metal bleachers.

III.

You walk through your gardens,
farmer, witnessing crops;
you name plants, show me
how to harvest.

IV.

You mold me into
a potter spinning clay
in circles,
shaping bowls and vases.

V.

Now, full-grown,
like a tree rooted deep,
I bend forward into the light
of your voice in prayer.

—Lenard D. Moore,
    from FOREVER HOME

FATHER'S PLEDGE

Long before the Million Man March, in October 1995, poet, educator, and publisher Haki R. Madhubuti (born Don L. Lee in 1942) penned this "Father's Pledge" for black fathers everywhere. His words rest directly on the pulse of every paternal principle in my book.

1. I will work to be the best father I can be. Fathering is a daily mission, and there are no substitutes for good fathers. Since I have not been taught to be a father, in order to make my "on the job" training easier, I will study, listen, observe and learn from my mistakes.

2. I will openly display love and caring for my wife and children. I will listen to my wife and children. I will hug and kiss my children often. I will be supportive of the mother of my children and spend quality time with my children.

3. I will teach by example. I will try to introduce myself and my family to something new and developmental every week. I will help my children with their homework and encourage them to be involved in extracurricular activities.

4. I will read to or with my children as often as possible. I will provide opportunities for my children to develop creatively in the arts: music, dance, drama, literature and visual arts. I will challenge my children to do their best.

5. I will encourage and organize frequent family activities for the home and away from home. I will try to make life a positive adventure and make my children aware of their extended family.

6. I will never be intoxicated or "high" in the presence of my children; nor will I use language unbecoming for an intelligent and serious father.

7. I will be nonviolent in my relationships with my wife and children. As a father, my role will be to stimulate and encourage my children rather than carry "the big stick."

8. I will maintain a home that is culturally in tune with the best of African American history, struggle and future. This will be done, in part, by developing a library and record/disc, video, and visual art collections that reflect the developmental aspects of African people worldwide. There will be _order_ and _predictability_ in our home.

9. I will teach my children to be responsible, disciplined, fair and honest. I will teach them the importance of family, community, politics and economics. I will teach them the importance of the Nguzo Saba (Black value system) and the role that ownership of property and businesses play in our struggle.

10. As a father, I will attempt to provide my family with an atmosphere of love and security to aid them in their development into sane, loving, productive, spiritual, hard-working, creative African Americans who realize they have a responsibility to do well and help the less fortunate of this world. I will teach my children to be _activists_ and to _think_ for themselves.

INTRODUCTION

We are in need of illumination. Of bright light, and much of it.

For far too long, the images and memories of our fathers and forefathers have been obscured, misshapen. We have left them lurking and loitering in the shadows, like young men on a street corner milling about, unsure of their collective mission or their next move. They have been left standing onstage, squinting into an audience that sits unmoving and unmoved; the only indication that they see anything at all is the flicker of cynicism that dances across their faces as they sit. The air around them is not joyous; nor is it celebratory. It hangs heavy with the vestiges of a darkened history; a history and a heritage that I plan—with every ounce of strength within me—to celebrate and glorify within the pages of this book.

This is a book about black fathers. It is intended to celebrate black fathers and families; to yell "bravo" from the darkened corners of the theater; to stand up in grateful ovation, applauding with heart and happiness, offering encouragement, cheering their performance, healing hurt, and calling for an encore. Again and again.

If I have to drag a huge spotlight onto this darkened stage—even if it means scarring and scratching the polished floors of this darkened theater in an effort to illuminate the lives of these beautiful black men who are our fathers—I will do it happily and without reserve.

I know a bit about dragging out lights to illuminate the world around me.

I've tried valiantly to illuminate darkened corners before—literally—and there is one particular experience I am certain I'll never forget, which bears sharing:

A while back, during my high school years (we'll leave it at that), some girlfriends and I decided to host a soiree (translated: throw some Fritos in a bowl, borrow my sister's Earth, Wind & Fire eight-track, saturate ourselves with the mist-of-the-times called Jean Naté, and wait for our nervous, jittery male counterparts to arrive—at my house!). The party languished and lagged; we were too nervous and new to dance or even talk, and the shadow of my father's face loomed large in my mind as I imagined him walking through the door at any minute. In a nutshell, *we needed light that night;* light that would make us want to sway and swoon to the can't-resist-swaying-and-swooning rhythm of EW&F's "Reasons" and "That's the Way of the World," and maybe, if we felt bold enough, to actually establish eye contact with these beautiful brothers who fancied themselves young men.

I remember that night as I would a throbbing toothache. Our party was verging on palpable pain; the pain of embarrassment and inexperience and not knowing what to do to resuscitate this dying patient that was called our adolescence. That night, we were in dire need of brother Isaac.

As in Hayes.

As in just one precious droplet of his "hot, buttered soul."

In an effort to brighten the mood that night, I dragged my older sister's metal strobe light across the surface of my father's brand-new poker table, creating three long, deep scratches on its freshly polished surface so ugly and completely irreparable that I *still* wince every time I think about it. We needed light that night; an incandescent, celebratory light to breathe life into our gasping soiree—and I did my best to create it, whatever the risk.

In my mind, we still need that light today. That illumination. That glowing light that casts itself into darkened corners and brightens everything around it. And we need to search for it. Drag it out from someplace. Scratch the surface if necessary in an effort to get it.

So, years later, I'm dragging out my light again, because we are in need of its brightness. It will be a light so bright that moths will flitter and flutter in its periphery and dust particles will dance in its path. Its lighted path will bathe our black fathers in the glory and grace they deserve and, for too long, have gone without.

Although I interviewed many people for this book, the light that illuminated my path most brightly as I wrote emanates from a flame that still burns brightly in my own heart.

That flame is my father.

In this book, I draw heavily on personal, paternal reflections and memories that bathe me in a light so warm and intense that something in me whispers that my father must still be walking somewhere on this earth. Since his death, I am struck more by Daddy's spiritual presence than by his physical absence. As I wrote this book, my father paid me several spiritual visits that made my heart shine and my spirit smile. He guided my hand, looking tenderly over my shoulder as I wrote, patting me lightly as the words and wisdom came together in the form of this book.

But this "light"—filled with boundless joy and immeasurable respect for black fathers everywhere—does not belong to me alone. It is a shared spotlight, created collectively by all of the people I interviewed, sat down with, excerpted quotes from, and spoke with on the telephone; by all of the people who shared with me their scribbled notes, scrawled letters, treasured photographs, and childhood memories on the subject of their own fathers and the broader topic of black fatherhood itself.

Not all of the memories are happy. Some are tearstained and painful. But the beauty and promise of this book lie in the fact that even—perhaps especially—in the midst of our sometimes painful, muffled memories and in the shadow of our bitter struggles, the black father emerges bent, but not broken. His spirit may sag heavily on one page, but soar, heavenward, on the next. In every chapter, his strength and tenacity are celebrated and applauded, intricately and deliberately woven into every shared experience. Even the painful ones.

For hundreds of years our fathers and forefathers struggled, wandered, tried to escape the injustice and indignity that slashed long slices across their faces like a bitter wind, cutting deep into the hearts of the wives and the children whom they fought so hard to protect. Although those historically bitter winds have subsided to a degree, what remains—or what *should* remain—is our desire to uplift and praise those men in our lives who sacrificed and swallowed so much of their pride. What *should* remain is a hunger; a hollering that comes deep from within our souls, for our fathers to rejoin the family fold and to reassert their rightful, historic place of prominence on the family mantel.

And always, there is the light:

First and foremost, the light of our Lord God, who so gently bandaged the bruised and bloodied wounds of our past and relieved us—gradually and on His own time—of the ravages of slavery and bondage. It is this heavenly Father I celebrate early in my book, along with an invitation for every one of us to lift both our heavenly and our earthly fathers up, together, in noisy, uncompromising, faith-filled praise! For without a keen eye trained, always, toward our Heavenly Father, how in the world will our souls know the glory and greatness of our *earthly* fathers? The earthly father and the Heavenly Father are inextricably bound. To survive as a people, we must become more mindful and appreciative of this beautiful bond, for it has been given to us as a precious gift. Black fathers who can learn to incorporate our Heavenly Father not only into their own lives, but also into the lives of their children, are giving their families the gift of a lifetime. It is the gift of infinite love, boundless mercy, humility, faith, and the promise of forgiveness.

There is another light that I pray illuminates the words in this book:

This light is wider and more all-encompassing than a mere spotlight. This light is more of a searchlight; its reach is diffuse and far-reaching. It settles comfortably upon everything in its path, like the golden dust a magician blows from the palm of his hand or like the "bear hugs" my father used to wrap us up in the moment he got home from work each day. Daddy's wide, wise embrace never settled on any one of us in particular, but somehow showered over all seven of us as a collective group. How comforted and buoyed we were by his closeness and the promise of his paternal presence! How fortified and strengthened we were by the light of our father's love, which washed over us in waves, like a summer rain shower! It is my intention to invite the reader to come with me and bask in this diffuse, dappled sunlight.

The chapters that examine and celebrate the black father as provider, protector, and friend all lend themselves to such basking: it is a journey that each of us can take by reaching back into the personal recesses of our own memories and by gaining strength and sustenance from the shared memories of our own childhoods; when the black community was strong and values such as honor, integrity, and personal accountability kept us closely bound within a safe, collective embrace.

An important literary development as I wrote this book, whose initial, sole focus was to be upon the black father: it became impossible for me to examine—much less celebrate—black fathers without examining the over-all state of the black family unit as well. Fathers do not exist in isolation. Implicit in the very definition of the word "father" is the notion that he is connected to someone other than himself; that he is bound by his own progeny; part of a larger family unit. This book is about fathers, but its embrace has to encompass the larger structure of the black family as well.

There is a final light that exists within the pages of my book.

It is a beacon.

A single, solitary beacon whose light does not emanate from above, like the spotlight shining downward upon a single subject; nor does it cast itself in a circular, rotating glow like a searchlight. Rather, its trajectory is level, parallel not only with the earth but with our earthly, daily circumstances. This beacon of light cuts straight through the darkness, inviting those who are lost, weary, or off course to find their way back home to their fathers, back to the safety and certainty of solid ground. Like the lighthouse beacon that guides lost seafaring ships back to land by shining bright light through foggy, murky nights, *Black Fathers: A Call for Healing* will, hopefully, offer a similarly outstretched hand to families and fathers who have somehow drifted off course.

The closing chapter on healing and forgiveness, along with the personal anecdotes from people who themselves have been healed or who have experienced the humility of paternal or familial forgiveness, generates enough wattage to light up the world. These testimonials are rays of light that sing songs of redemption, songs of peace, songs of forgiveness. They hum and harmonize and extend a graceful, faith-filled invitation for fathers and families to heal.

I, for one, am weary of watching so many of our fathers and our black men linger unceremoniously in the shadows; not only in the shadows of two centuries of racism, rage, and prejudice, but the subliminal, sour shadows that are created every time we open a newspaper and see the obituary pages filled with photos of young black men who *could* have been fathers—had they lived long enough; who *could* have been the vital links in a weakening chain that is the black family unit; who could have been *taught* to be good fathers, but whose chances were somehow snuffed out, along with their futures and their lives.

Where is the celebration in that? Where is the honor and redemption in these painful images? And how do we get back to the brighter days, when fathers and families were bound by an unconditional, collective love that was larger than our own individual interests and existence?

Black Fathers is a call for a return to the days of yesterday, where tradition, honor, and rock-hard core values were the resin that bound our families and communities so closely together. Where discipline and commitment and a collective need for survival lit our pathway, and we were unembarrassed and unafraid of facing a world where right was right and wrong was wrong. There were no gray areas, and our children knew it. Our grip was firm, and our children not only appreciated that strong, sure grip, but survived because of it.

Another component of my book, a theme that settled solidly into my heart very early in the writing process, has to do with hands: strong, loving hands that we can wrap around our shoulders as we would a heavy velvet cloak on a chilly day. The holding of hands. The intertwining of a father's large fingers through his child's tiny ones, like a father bear holding his cub's little paw. Hands that clasp, palm to palm, in heavenly prayer. Hands that uplift, strengthen, and mold. Hands—your own hands, those of you who are holding this book at this very minute—that will remix the cement that will allow us to pour a strong new foundation for black fathers and families everywhere.

Because loving hands helped mold my words as I wrote, you will see various visual images of fathers holding hands with their children: a photo of my own father holding my hand as I grasped his for strength and support on a hot, sunny day in July almost two decades ago—the day that I married my best friend; the image of my son holding his father's hand as he sits atop his knee, holding tightly not only for balance, but for the promise of his father's strong, responsive grip as they kneel near a window at Tavern on the Green in New York City; an anonymous father with his toddler son, both dressed alike, holding hands at a summer festival, smiling with love and pride and the sheer happiness that comes from simply being together. And on the back cover, me, a six-year-old ponytail-wearing happy little girl with one hand near my mouth and the other wrapped securely in my father's large, loving hand.

This is a book where hands—*all* of our hands—will heartily applaud the unsung heroes who are our fathers. Ours are the hands that will reach boldly into the darkness, find that electric switch, and flick it upward so that this theater that is our lives can again be bathed in bright light and we can, at long last, look at our fathers—and our families—and smile.

So take my hand and let's walk this celebratory paternal road together. No matter that I am a woman and a mother writing a highly personalized book about black fathers. To be sure, my grip on the issue will be just as firm; my fingers will intertwine around and through yours just as tightly as we examine together the topic of black fatherhood. No, I cannot speak with a man's voice or a father's voice. But the light I hope to shine in this book can bathe all of us—man, woman, father, wife—in a collective glow that knows no gender.

Why?

Because the only way we will improve and assure our future is to stop for a moment to still our souls, listen closely to our own inner voices and to the wisdom of others, and begin moving away from this growing darkness: toward the light.

My voice is that of a woman and a mother. But I have known, deep in my own heart, the spirit and grace of a man who was my father.

The time has come (and gone) for a ringing celebration of our brothers; of our brethren; our fathers, no matter what darkened roads they may have walked in the past. Given that we celebrate Mother's Day with such syrupy sweet sentimentalism and warmth, what has happened to the celebration of the black father? Why aren't restaurants filled to capacity on Father's Day in the same way they are on Mother's Day? Why aren't all the phone lines, fax machines, and answering machines jammed all the day long on Father's Day from so many millions of African American children calling their fathers just to say "I love you" and "I'm so blessed to have you in my life"? Where is the ringing affirmation for black fathers everywhere?

Listen. Can you hear it? It's the unsettling, searing sound of silence.

This is not the placid, peaceful sound of silence that we all long for when we want to escape from the noisy clamor of our lives. No. It is a silence that needs to be broken up with clanging cymbals, noisy affirmations, and maybe even a little bit of foot-stomping. Foot-stomping for our fathers.

Now, *there's* some noise we need to be making.

Kristin Clark Taylor

1.

THE BEAUTY OF
"BEING THERE"

A CLARION CALL TO BLACK FATHERS:
YOUR PRESENCE IS MANDATORY!

"My son is the flame in my heart. . . .
How could I live in a world without him?"

—GEORGE SANKER,
DIRECTOR OF BEST MEN, INC.

We are in need of our fathers. Our stomachs are growling, hungry for their presence. Our throats are parched, thirsty for the moment, the minute, the second they walk back into our lives, bringing the smiles and certainty and solidity that only a father can provide.

Our fathers of yesterday—and the countless faceless fathers of today who too often go unnoticed and unappreciated—are the reason we need to rejoice. These strong black men were and are the backbone of the family unit, holding things together as the stress and strain of daily life does all it can to stretch and tear apart the fabric of our family lives. These are the men we celebrate. These are the fathers we thank.

That being said, there still exists a gaping hole where our fathers used to stand, stalwart and strong, at the epicenter of our lives. It is a hole that seems to be growing deeper and darker; a hole that represents their alarming absence and swallows up our young black children, leaving them angry, despondent, and "hurting like when you get the wind knocked out of you," as one young man described it to me. A hole that forces single black mothers, strong and resourceful as they may be, to play a dual role that is physically and emotionally impossible: the roles of both father and mother simultaneously. The two-in-one parent. As dedicated, determined, and flexible as many of my single sister-mothers are, they cannot be fathers. I will not—cannot—mince words, struggle for verbiage that is genteel and inoffensive, or dance daintily around the ugliness of the absentee father. But I can offer shared quotes, personal stories, and inspiring life lessons that I've received from others during the writing of this book, which redeem and uplift those fathers who *are* there. Who *do* care. Who somehow manage to blend and balance the qualities of courage, leadership, and authority with compassion, gentleness, humility, and respect. Who reach out to their child during both the happy and the sad times, or when the one thing that child wants more than anything in the world is to hold his daddy's hand and secure that special place in his heart.

The absence of the black father speaks volumes about our larger society in general and about our black community in particular. These fatherless children do not know the unique and comforting joy of having the man who is their father simply "be there" at their side. Through no fault of their own, these children cannot savor—or even look forward to—the promise of their father's embrace or a goodnight kiss on the forehead when the day is done and the cream-colored crescent moon hangs from its invisible thread in the sky.

But therein lies the joy: there is no doubt that the sun has darkened our familial skies, but it has not yet disappeared completely behind the horizon. To those black fathers who are already there, praise be to you. But to those who have strayed, you can again "be there" for your children, to lead them and guide them, before the setting of the sun. It will require a fundamental change in the way we define our priorities and a careful reexamination of the tools we employ to gauge the depth of our faith in fatherhood, but it can be done.

Remember our fathers of yesterday? The ones who worked hard at good-paying jobs and brought home their paychecks to provide for their wives and their children? Who cherished the sacred institution of marriage and taught their children the difference between right and wrong—even if it meant an occasional slap on the backside or a voice raised in anger? The ones who instilled the values of valor, dignity, honesty, and accountability into the hearts and minds of their children through their own thoughts, words, and deeds? Where staying in one place, under one roof, with one family didn't mean—as many young people think today—that they are "stuck in a rut" but, rather, cocooned within the comfort of a safe, stable home and peaceful harbor?

Martin Luther King, Jr., saw black America's families and fathers slowly ripping apart at the seams as well—but he, like me, believed in redemption, rejuvenation, and rehabilitation. The ravages of racism—the bitter taste of a history that enslaved our black men and shackled their feet as well as their pride—was the first great rip at our familial fabric. But through faith, fearlessness, and sacrifice, we somehow managed to keep our families together—and it was the black father who was the primary strength: the resin, the provider and protector who helped keep us intact.

———◆———

Dr. King's words echo in my mind:

"The Negro family is scarred; it is submerged,
but it struggles to survive."

———◆———

If I could roll the pages of this book into the shape of a foghorn or a makeshift trumpet with which to issue my clarion call, I would. I'd make a loud sound, a sound that takes us back to the days of yesterday and is steeped in the safety of security and tradition. We cannot stress the importance of a father "being there" for his children until we can identify the reasons that so many of them vanished in the first place.

Sadly, the notion of the traditional nuclear black family has all but vanished, and what has vanished with it, particularly as it relates to our fathers, are words we used to hold dear:

Love.

Honor.

Respect.

Accountability.

I'd love to simply say, "Let's open the dictionary and find those words again and paste them all over our hearts and soak them into our spirits and spread thick coats—just as we would a fresh new can of paint or a roll of beautiful new wallpaper—all over those fathers who, for whatever reason, can't 'be there' for their children."

But the solution is not so simple.

How in the world can a child love, honor, and respect a father who is absent from his life? One way is to draw from the strengths and rock-hard family values of yesterday, when integrity, stability, honor, and discipline— you know the kind of discipline I mean, that "look sideways at your mother like that again and I'll take my belt off" kind of discipline—stood for something.

This chapter calls us home. It urges black families to get together in love and laughter. And in my opinion, the best way to get back to the "way it used to be" is to reestablish the values that were cemented in us when we were children: values that had to do with *both* parents playing vital, visual roles in their children's spiritual and emotional development; where fathers led by example, positioned themselves as the standard-bearers; where their assured paternal presence was absolute and predictable.

Listen.

Can you hear it?

It's my call, my trumpet sound. In the form of a poem, written in the language of Malink'e (spoken in the Ivory Coast of Africa), that epitomizes all the joy and jubilation a child feels for the father whose presence looms large in his life. I share it now as a celebratory tribute to all the black fathers who stand close to their children, the black fathers who see their highest calling as one of "being there" for their children, showering them with love and bathing them in light. To you, beautiful fathers, these words speak. And to those who aren't or can't be there for their families, these words invite:

Baba E kokandigne'
Baba M'bi le'le' Bognan
Baba M'bi le'le' Barahou
Baba M'bi le'le' Sarata
Baba E le' Minan N' la Fongnonan

Translated:

Father, it is you who I love
Father, it is you I respect
Father, it is you who I honor
Father, it is you who I need
Father, it is you whom I look up to
Father, it is you who gave me life.

Now, let's make a joyful noise to the fathers who are there, and extend a loving, healing hand to those who aren't.

For too many black men, fatherhood has become optional. Debatable. Expendable. Discretionary. Somewhere along the line, we forgot that this thing called "fatherhood" is not a value-added enhancement, nor is it an option to be exercised at the will or discretion of the interested party. Fatherhood is not a spontaneous, spur-of-the-moment afterthought. It's not an enhanced service like call waiting or a dry cleaner that delivers.

As the song says, "our children are our future," living, breathing, vulnerable creatures who laugh when they're happy, bleed when they're pricked, tremble when they're frightened, and cry big, salty tears when they're sad.

Too many of our black children today are not merely "sad" about the absence of their father in their daily lives.

They are dying from it.

They are our walking wounded: lonely, angry, and confused. They are being cheated out of their own childhood, the edges of their lives singed and the center of their hearts scorched by being forced, for whatever reason, to grow up in a world without Daddy.

A few points of clarification are in order: I'm obviously not saying that every black child is at risk or every black father is at fault. I hold fast to the belief and celebrate the fact that there are more responsible, responsive fathers out there than there are absentee fathers. Nor is it my intention to undermine the superhuman efforts of single mothers who are raising their children just fine, thank you, in a world without their fathers. But it is also my strong belief that a return to the fundamental values that we used to cherish—and now that I think about it, probably took for granted at the time—will give us the compass we need to get our families, and the faith of our fathers, back on track.

Now that we've dispensed with those important clarifications, let's move right to the middle of the madness: a dual definition of the word "mad" that includes both "angry" and "insane." Because that is what black fathers who are "missing in action" and who are playing the cruel "hide-and-seek" game with their children are creating: a mad, angry, insane world where their children must take a backseat and hope for the best, which is too often the worst.

To those fathers—and there are many—who are there for their children, who ask questions at the PTA meetings, read *Green Eggs and Ham* to their child on a rainy Sunday afternoon, and leave work early to make it to their daughter's soccer game, I hope you can hear my hands clapping in raucous applause. To produce a healthy, well-adjusted child who will eventually grow into a stable, well-balanced adult who can skillfully navigate these choppy, turbulent waters we call life, you must be there to provide ballast and direction in your child's life. You must be there to provide your children not only with a compass, but with an anchor. You must be there not only to help keep the wind in their sails, but the hope in their hearts.

You must be there.

Unless you are imprisoned, incapacitated, or legally prohibited from seeing the children whom you helped create and bring into this world, your presence in their lives is not merely a warm, fuzzy abstraction. It is mandatory. As mandatory as the air we need to fill our lungs; as the water we need to quench our thirst; as the love that God showers over us, even when we're not looking, which He, in turn, expects us to shower over others (particularly our progeny).

With that said, my mind has cleared a bit. We can now move past the middle of the madness that "invisible fathers" seem to breed. Now we can look past the bitterness to the beauty: the beauty that flows from a father simply "being there" for his child.

———

And if divorce or separation is unavoidable and imminent,
listen to the words of this loving brother who still
cherishes his time with his daughter:

"I treat my visitation rights like gold.
If I am scheduled to pick up my daughter at 3:00 P.M.
to go to a movie or something, I get there at 2:45."
—EARL OFARI HUTCHINSON, AUTHOR AND FATHER

———

Here is a brother—a father—whose marriage didn't work but whose love for his daughter remains as solid as a rock, and the moments he spends with her, in his own words are more precious than gold. So even though he's no longer sharing the same roof with his daughter, he's still sharing his soul—as well as the promise of his presence.

A wonderful man named George Sanker is a shining example of black fatherhood at its best. He and brothers like him are why we celebrate all that is good about black fathers.

As the director of a national organization called Best Men, Inc., Sanker offers definition and development to young African American males in an attempt to mold them into responsible adults and, as a natural outgrowth, faithful fathers. The mission of Best Men: to provide boys with the tools and an environment that will help them acquire a clear picture of what it means to be a man.

Their work offers a healing hand to at-risk males, predominantly African American, who may be (or who may *feel*) fatherless and who have, for some reason or another, simply veered off track. How does Best Men help young men acquire a clear picture of what it means to be a man? The organization's own mission: by implementing a multifaceted program that not only teaches boys right and wrong, but provides them with a community of men of character and peers who will support and encourage them in their desire to become men worthy of respect.

Sanker's spirit is similar to mine. He, too, wants to bring back the traditionalism and values of our past. In his mind, as in mine, the existence of the black family unit (and the father's position within that unit) depends on it. He responds honestly and directly to my call to fathers:

"Let's face it: you can invite the black father back into the family unit and urge him to reassert himself into his child's life, and your invitation may sound beautiful; even poetic, but it's *hard*. [The problem] must be looked at realistically if it is to be solved. If a divorced or absentee father suddenly tries to come back into his child's life, it could become a battle; imbalanced and protracted. Sure, he can cherish those court-ordered moments or hours or days he has with his child, but he cannot assert his full, round-the-clock authority as a father because it has been taken away from him: legally, emotionally, and physically."

Sanker, himself a happily married African American father, continues, digging straight to the root of the larger problem. I listen to him as he speaks, an authoritative, paternal male voice who upholds the values of traditionalism: "In order to invite those black fathers who are out of the home back into their families' lives, we have to look at a much, much larger picture. We have to look at the value of the institution of marriage," he says definitively.

"Marriage—and staying married—needs to be our center focus; our top priority. From that, all else will fall naturally. Marriage, in itself, is what helps young men become *true* men. Because the very context of marriage enlarges a man's vision and perspective. I know it did for me. It expanded my vision so dramatically that it's difficult to explain in words. Instead of 'my' concerns, it's become 'our' concerns. Instead of 'what's right for me,' it's now 'what is right for my family.'

"In today's modern world," he says, "you see lots of single heads of household and even same-sex marriages. We, as black men and fathers, have to encourage a more traditional view; that a child needs a mother *and* a father who are committed to each other, who are willing to scrape through—and survive—the hard bumps that come with any marriage; who respect and love one another. Young black boys need to see more of our men 'being there' and trying to make things work. Unless they see it themselves, within their own family structure, they won't learn to value it in their own lives."

Amen and amen again, I think, as he speaks. Because he speaks not only from his heart, but from his uniquely male experience. Sanker speaks directly from his personal base of knowledge. When it comes to faithful fatherhood, he's been there. Done that.

He continues:

"Too many young black men are blind to the fact that there really *are* good, strong, value-driven two-parent families. Unfortunately, they think it's an anomaly; something off of television or in books. What they see is perhaps their own mother and father who are not married—*they just have children together*. The father comes around every once in a while, but he lives in his house, and she lives in hers; and too often the child is made to live in between. The question becomes, How do we uproot some of these disturbing norms and revalue a higher level of accountability and responsibility for men, where they finally understand that making babies and leaving their children is not the honorable thing to do? Not only is it dishonorable, but it is shameful."

Sanker shifts focus slightly. "Let me speak carefully: I am not casting judgments or aspersions—I devote my life to guiding young men in the right direction. I'm simply saying that we, fathers and families—long ago— used to have something that worked. For us to return to that model, to me, is basic common sense. These things that I've mentioned, in my mind, are what will place the black father back [in] his position of authority, respect, and leadership."

Sanker's passion pours from his own childhood experience. His father, he says, "wasn't there for me when I was growing up."

Sadness shades his voice, but bitterness does not.

"My father was a hardworking man, but he just wasn't there for me. When I became a father, it was very difficult for me to establish the positive, loving patterns of fatherhood because I hadn't known them personally myself. I had to work at it; to *learn* it from friends and mentors.

"My son, Kendrick, is the light of my life," he says with love so thick in his voice you could cut it with a butter knife.

"I love being a father, and I love, as you say, Kristin, 'being there' for my son. Fatherhood, for me, is a character-building, faith-filled experience. And having a life partner who I love who is my wife helps bolster our family unit. Through both marriage and fatherhood, I have learned humility. When I make a mistake with my son or my wife, I have learned to say, 'I'm sorry. I was wrong'—and to ask them for forgiveness. When Kendrick sees me doing this, he doesn't see my humility as a sign of weakness—because it's not—he sees it as a sign of strength, which it is.

"When I compromise or disagree with my wife, or when I stumble, *Kendrick sees me get back up,* and even at his young age, I think he is comforted somehow; not necessarily by the fact that he sees me stumble, but that when I *do*, he sees me getting right back up. He sees, by my actions, that it's okay to make mistakes—as long as you get back up and correct them. I don't think he sees my occasional stumbling as relinquishing my authority as a father at all. Instead, it reminds him, through his father's actions, that I am not invincible—and neither is he. And he sees how I put him and my wife first in my life. These are the qualities I hope he latches onto and passes down to his own children."

Qualities indeed. Qualities that need to simmer slowly in our souls, with *both* parents constantly stirring the pot.

When are the times that I needed my father most? On my first day of nursery school, which I remember as vividly as this morning's breakfast: I sat nestled so closely to Daddy in the front seat of our station wagon that I might as well have been sitting on his lap. Butterflies were fluttering so furiously in my stomach that I was certain a Monarch would fly straight out of my mouth. My wool jumper was scratchy against my skinny legs and the band on my ponytail was too tight. But as soon as we arrived at the school and got out of the car, Daddy reached down and wrapped his big bear paw around my tiny hand, and the dance of the butterflies stopped. I was still nervous, but I knew that in a few hours Daddy would be picking me up—not only from that new school that smelled like Dial soap and Pinesol, but into his arms—and that everything would be okay again. Why? Because he told me so. Because his grace and his grip told me as much. And he *did* come back. On that first day, I sat in the corner of the classroom quietly, drawing my father a picture of an apple, not only because he loved apples, but because I was too shy to reach across the table for any other crayon but the one I had, which was red. "Candy Apple Red." Just as he'd promised, Daddy appeared at the classroom door at the end of the school day almost magically, with an outstretched hand reaching toward me again, and together, we climbed back into our station wagon and drove home.

God smiled on me when he gave me Daddy. He was a loving father who was loved by all seven of his children. And he was "there" for all seven of his children.

This tells me that it can still be done.

Another time I needed Dad's strength and paternal presence was, as one might imagine, on my wedding day. He and my mother, Mary Elizabeth Clark, had flown in from Detroit a few days before the ceremony and for some reason, even in the midst of the hubbub, I lingered around them closely, not letting either of them move too far out of my vision. The day before the wedding, Daddy made an unusual complaint about not feeling very well. Mother, myself, and all of my siblings checked his temperature by feeling his forehead, his cheeks, and his neck with the backs of our hands; maybe a low-grade fever, but nothing to worry about. Mostly, he just looked sad. Forlorn.

Lonnie, the wonderful man who was to become my husband in a matter of hours, gave me back to my father for the last time by suggesting Daddy and I take a drive, just to be together. Shortly after we pulled out of the driveway, I could feel his soul begin to smile again. We sat in comfortable silence until he was ready to speak.

"I guess I'll be giving you away tomorrow, Baby Girl," he said as we

I needed to hold Dad's hand on my wedding day

drove past the White House and weaved our way through the traffic of Pennsylvania Avenue.

"This time tomorrow, Lonnie will be my son-in-law; and you will be the most beautiful bride in the world."

But as the wedding day dawned, I could see that Daddy really wasn't feeling well. He wore a pinched, pained look on his face as we stood in the basement of the church moments before the ceremony. Even his boutonniere seemed to hang, limp and lifeless, from the lapel of his tuxedo. My sister Joann noticed his mood, too, and tried to cheer him up.

"Well, this is the day that your baby girl grows up!" Jo said with a smile, straightening the back of my gown, with Mother adjusting my veil and trying to brighten up the moment.

Dad looked as if he was going to throw up.

He responded to Jo, but looked at me: "She'll always be my baby girl," Dad said with the glimmer of a smile. "I guess now she'll be someone *else's* baby, too."

I don't think he was brooding. Only contemplating. Reflecting.

At the reception, when it came time for the bride to dance with her father, he held my hand close and glided me across the room. I'd never felt so safe or anchored in my life. Daddy was there when I needed him most. Although he'd given me away, his paternal grip remained firm and unwavering. And as we danced, I held his hand as tightly. As tightly as I would have held a life preserver.

The vital importance of a father "being there" for his children spans the generations and crosses the barriers of time. For this chapter, once again, God Himself took me by the hand and led me straight to a miracle of a man named Mr. Dwight F. Holloway, Sr., a distinguished church elder and a senior deacon at Emmanuel Baptist Church in Washington, D.C.

Well into his ninth decade of life, Mr. Holloway still remembers clearly the fact that his father's presence was what made a vital difference during his childhood.

"I grew up in the country, in a rural county in Virginia called Lunenberg," he says to me in a soft, dignified voice. He speaks slowly not because his speech is in any way hindered by his advanced age, but because his thought process is incredibly detailed, his memories as vivid and vibrant as they probably were during his youth.

Here is a man who will not be rushed.

"There was never a time I can remember when my father *wasn't* there for me," Mr. Holloway reflects.

"Back when I was growing up, it was nothing to see a family of ten or twelve children," he remembers. "But there were only four of us, which was a small family back then."

Two brothers and a sister.

"We had our own farm, which was rare that long ago," Brother Deacon says slowly.

"I'm not bragging or putting on airs, but my father made sure the land we lived on and the crops we produced were things we owned outright," he says with pride. "Everyone who lived around us were sharecroppers, but the fact that we owned our land gave us a certain faith and flexibility that many of the families around us just didn't have."

A wise man, just as his father must have been.

"The fact that my father owned his land actually allowed him to spend more time with his family," he said. "I don't mean to say that he'd sit around rocking in a chair on the porch or standing in the fields talking the day away, but I mean to try to make the point that the only person he had to answer to was himself.

"We all worked hard on the farm, but if my father had some business to take care of in town or if he wanted to carry us somewhere in the horse and buggy, he didn't have to check with anybody to see if it was okay or get permission from somebody to take the time off. He just *did it*."

Deacon Holloway's spirit shines through the telephone. Or maybe it's the memory of his own father's spirit that is creating such warmth and light. Probably both.

"Owning his own land didn't give my father any more time with me, you understand," he says. "But it did give him more discretion as to how he spent his time. And since it was obviously *his choice* to spend time with his children and teach us how to work the land and become skilled, we'd spend many, many hours together."

Mr. Holloway continues, "What this means is that my father *chose* to spend time with his family. In those days, it wasn't even a decision. It was a given."

Bingo. Therein lies the difference.

Fatherhood, in the deacon's day, wasn't an option or an inconvenience to be cast back into the sea like yesterday's catch. Fatherhood, then, wasn't perceived as a lifetime prison sentence or as a legal and financial burden whose proof could be determined with any certainty only by a DNA test. No. In the deacon's day, fatherhood was a badge of honor, worn proudly, without reserve.

"Even when I was a small boy, my father would let me help him plow the fields or harvest the crops. Whatever it was, we did it *together*," Deacon Holloway remembers.

"My life was guided by and inspired by what my father—*and* my mother—provided for me. And to me, his mere presence was just about all I needed. He was a proud man, and a good father," says Holloway.

While I'm on the phone with Deacon Holloway, my daughter, Mary Elizabeth, ambles into the room carrying a cellophane bag of Hershey's Kisses, holding up two fingers with a "just two pieces and I'll put the bag away" expression on her face. (Brother Deacon, as I mentioned, is not a man to be interrupted or rushed. Mary Elizabeth is my own, living chocolate kiss, and I love her more than air and water and even chocolate, but Deacon was beginning to preach, and I didn't want to miss a word of it.) I wave my daughter away dismissively as I listen to Deacon continue, hoping the crackle of the cellophane doesn't distract him or impede the fluidity of his thought. "*Eat them all*," I mouth to my daughter, nodding my head in silent, enthusiastic approval. She turns on her heels in happiness and mild shock, recognizing now that I'm on the phone with someone obviously very, very important. I hear the cellophane bag being ripped open as she moves down the hall, and I say a quick, silent prayer to God, asking Him to forgive me my maternal irresponsibility, to spare my child the certain tummy ache she'll get if she eats that entire bag of chocolate kisses, and to impart upon her—if it is His will—the desire to eat only two or three pieces, rather than the entire bag.

Deacon Holloway has a theory—a solution, if you will—that if black families *spent more time together and less time arguing, divorcing, and fighting in courtrooms about who gets or even wants custody of the children*, it would make a positive difference. He emphasizes the fact that the art of families socializing together has become, tragically, a thing of the past.

I agree.

When did taking a family walk after dinner become an "uncool" thing to do? For that matter, when did having the entire family sit down for dinner at the same time become such a rarity in our rushed, revolving worlds? Do the board games my husband pulls out from the closet make my children's eyes roll in boredom? As a matter of fact, no—at least, as of this writing, not yet. Our evening time is our most magical. It's uninterrupted family time that pulls us closer together in spirit.

The deacon continues: "What black families used to know how to do that they seem to have forgotten along the way is to have *fun* with themselves, with their friends, and with each other," he says. "Plain, simple fun that brings families together. You know, a summer social at the church on a Saturday night or when the men in town would take their sons down to the lake to fish on Sunday afternoons."

Again, his mind harkens back to his warm childhood days.

"My father made sure we had such fun when we were together!" he says with new energy and a light chuckle in his voice. Even through the phone I can feel him sitting up straighter in his chair.

"We worked *hard* in those fields of his—but we had fun, too."

Here, Mr. Holloway shares with me a beautiful family tradition that they used to keep friendships alive and family members united:

Quilting bees.

"I can remember when the corn was ready to be harvested, we'd have what you call a 'corn-shucking party.' All the neighbors from far and wide would come together on the farm that was about to harvest their crop, to help shuck the corn, because it was a big, big job."

I visualize a silhouette moving slowly along the horizon; a silhouette of fathers, mothers, and children walking together toward one farm; fathers holding the hands of their children, mothers carrying their babies, all on their way to a "corn-shucking" and a quilting bee.

"Once all that corn was ready to be shucked, we'd pull it into the middle of the field and gather it into one large pile. Mostly the men and their sons would shuck it and toss it into the bins. Nobody seemed to mind the work—even the smallest of the boys—because they were with their fathers and their families."

He creates a magical place where fathers and their children smile together, even—and especially—during their work.

"The women and wives would come, too, from far and wide. While we were shucking, the women were quilting. Quilting and talking and laughing until tears would come to their eyes."

A notion so sweet and simple in its purity that hot tears sting my own eyes.

Deacon continues, "The women would gather either outside the barn or in a large room. Everyone would bring pieces of cloth, rags, scraps of clothing—whatever they could find. If it was clean, it could be used to make a quilt. They'd put up these huge racks big enough to fill an entire room, and together, they'd create and stitch these beautiful quilts. Some women would be sewing, others would be cooking, others would be minding the children, but they all would be talking," he says with a smiling voice.

"It was a social time. We were just *glad to be together.* The men were glad because the corn had been shucked. The women were glad to be with each other. The children felt special; as if they performed a very important task and also had the chance to travel to another county on a 'trip.' Our families, then, had this wonderful sense of being together."

I remind myself to look up the art of quilting on the Internet. Can something like this, as a simple social example, be reintroduced into today's society in order to bring families back together? Can we re-create the yearning for togetherness and belonging that once burned so brightly in the lives of black families? Can our fathers come together in the name of a common cause and enjoy not only the work involved, but the collective joy of fellowship with their families?

I hang up the phone and set off in search of my daughter, whom I find downstairs, sitting at the kitchen table, head bent in concentration, two or three chocolate kisses lined in a neat row beside her math book. (She'd taped the rest of the bag shut, I observed with pride.)

She looks up at me, her father's—and my father's—features flashing across her face.

"Who were you talking to on the phone?" she asks curiously.

"A very wise man who loved his father very, very much," I answer.

"Like you loved Daddy Jim?" she asks, referring to my own father. (It was a nickname that all of his grandchildren used.) "And kind of how Lonnie Paul and I love Dad?"

I regard her for a moment, sitting there at the table, waiting for my answer.

"Yep," I say with more of a pursed-lip smile and a nod than a firm answer, because I was trying to stem tears. "Just like I loved Daddy Jim and just how the two of you love Daddy."

I realize, standing there in our kitchen, how blessed I am to have children who can so effortlessly identify with the universal notion of paternal love. It is no stranger to them. They know the feel of a father's love. They love their father in large, gulping doses.

And he loves them right back.

But I'll let my children speak, at this point, for themselves. Both teenagers, theirs are voices that need to be heard.

See That Man in the Front Row Wearing the Suit and the Smile? That's My Dad!

I love my father's scratchy beard (when he has one). It's rough and prickly when he kisses me, but by now my cheeks are pretty much used to it. It used to kind of hurt my skin when I was little. But not anymore. Now I love it.

As I've said, I love my father very much. And I know he loves me and would do anything in the world for me. Here's what I like to think about when I think about my father: for as long as I've been in school plays, ballet recitals, or even in wind ensemble, Dad and Mom have always gotten front-row seats. Always. Here's how it works: My mom will get there hours early and help set things up.

Lonnie holding his most cherished Christmas gifts, Lonnie Paul and Mary Elizabeth

She'll usually bring a big purse, and as she helps set up, she'll start removing all of this stuff out of her bag; maybe a book, a piece of fruit, and a scarf or something, and she puts them on the front-row chairs to reserve the seats until my dad and brother can get there, too. I guess that's what you call teamwork.

Right before a performance, I usually peek out from behind the wings of the stage and the first thing I always see is my family sitting front row, center. My dad is usually looking over the program, wearing his shiny, polished shoes and a really nice suit. (I forgot to mention that he's very handsome, too.)

After ballet recitals, he'll present me with a bouquet of fresh flowers, usually tied with a bright satin ribbon. He's very tall, so every year he always thinks he's surprising me by pulling the flowers out from behind his back, but I can always see them. Always.

As I grow older (I'm thirteen years old now) I think my brother, Lonnie Paul, is beginning to remind me more of Dad, which is actually kind of cool, except when he takes it too far (like sometimes Lonnie Paul will "scold" me about something or try to use a stern voice like Dad's if he's angry). The fact is that my brother is only two years older than me, but he's already trying to imitate our father!

What's really nice about Lonnie Paul becoming so much like Daddy is that the best parts of my father are now being passed down to the next generation. It's exactly what I hope my own son would do (if I ever have one, which would be a very long time from now!).

And even though this will be years and decades away, I'll also make sure my husband and I get front-row seats to every one of our children's recitals!

as told by Mary Elizabeth Taylor, 13

Yet another, loving testimony from my oldest child—my sixteen-year-old son, Lonnie Paul, on the assuring, predictable presence of his father.

The Bridge

I can't think of a time when my father wasn't there for me. When I was younger, I think I probably might have taken his presence for granted. I assumed that his constant support and presence was how all dads were, just because that's how mine was. Now I realize that *all* dads are not as devoted.

There are numerous things I love about my father. I love the fact that he is extremely intelligent; not just in areas like law and politics, but about how things relate to each other in the universe. Over the years, he's taught me that it's important to want to know about things such as world history, politics, and global economies. It's extremely important to him that my sister and I want to learn about the world around us. Both he and my mom help make history come alive for us; particularly the history of our own heritage and our own ancestors.

A while ago, Dad arranged for all of us (him, my mom, my sister, and me) to travel with key civil rights leaders and several members of the U.S. Congress on a journey to Mobile, Selma, and Montgomery, Alabama; all three the birthplaces of the civil rights movement. We traveled with a congressional delegation and a group called Faith and Politics so that we could reenact and discuss some of the defining moments of that part of our history.

I remember Dad reaching out to hold my hand as we walked through the park in Mobile where, only forty years earlier, African American men, women, and children had been hosed down with fire hoses and attacked by police dogs, all because they were brave enough to demand justice in a nonviolent way. My father and I looked at the bare spots on many of the trees in that park, where the force of the water hoses had literally blown the bark off the tree trunks. We watched old videos and television footage of black children tumbling down the street, knocked over by the force of the fire hoses that were being sprayed directly onto them.

On that same trip, Dad and I walked together across the famous Edmund Pettus Bridge (the bridge that connects Selma and Montgomery), and he explained everything that had happened on that bridge during the original march forty years ago. Riding on the bus to Selma, we took some of the same routes as the Freedom Riders took in the sixties. On the bus, we watched a tape of the PBS documentary *Eyes on the Prize*, which explained and showed how blacks were mistreated and disrespected—even as they tried to cross the very bridge my father and I were about to cross in a matter of hours. In the film, U.S. Congressman John Lewis of Georgia led all the protestors across that bridge. It was an honor I'll never forget to be riding on the same bus with Congressman Lewis, and to hear firsthand his personal stories of the tragedies and injustices our people suffered.

There were about a hundred of us in the group altogether. As we marched across the Edmund Pettus Bridge, Dad linked his arm through mine and someone started singing "We Shall Overcome," just like in the documentary we'd just watched. Just like it happened in history.

Congressman Lewis, a friend of my father's and a role model to me, marched right beside us. The congressman spent a lot of time during that trip talking with me about the past. Our past. He described his own personal experiences as a Freedom Fighter, and the pain he went through.

At the Dexter Avenue Baptist Church, the church where Martin Luther King, Jr., was once pastor and the same church where the four little girls were killed by a bomb, my father held my hand as we sat in the pew listening to one of the women who was actually with those little girls on that Sunday morning. She was remembering that terrible morning, and I remember lots of the people with us were crying, including my mom. I also remember how safe I felt sitting there, holding my father's hand as she spoke. He didn't pat my hand or squeeze it or anything embarrassing like that. He just held it.

Crossing that bridge with my father was something I'll never forget. Not in a year or even in a thousand years.

Lonnie Paul Taylor II, 16

Lonnie and Lonnie Paul, as always, holding hands, 1992

So the faith of our fathers still rings strong and true. They are there to nurture and nestle their children. It is cause for singing and celebration. But as we sing, let us make our collective chorus even louder to include all black fathers, everywhere.

2.

PRAYING HANDS

HOW PRAYER SO BEAUTIFULLY BINDS THE EARTHLY FATHER AND THE HEAVENLY FATHER

---

*"Sometimes God has to get you alone by yourself
so he can talk to your head."*
—T. J. JAKES, PASTOR,
AUTHOR, AND MOTIVATIONAL SPEAKER

Now that the clarion call has been issued to all fathers everywhere, let us turn our attention to our highest calling: recognizing and praising our Creator and Savior. This chapter not only glorifies and uplifts our Heavenly Father, but it extends an outstretched hand to fathers everywhere to allow His glory to shine directly into their lives.

There is nothing more important, nothing more urgent.

How wondrous and comforting it is to recognize that we are not alone in this wild world! And for children in particular, how blessed we need to make them realize they are to have not only an *earthly* father, but a Heavenly Father as well!

Along with this pleasing realization comes paternal—and parental—responsibility: the responsibility of black fathers to strengthen and celebrate the link between themselves, their children, and their God. Purposefully placing our children in His direct, divine path is a responsibility second to none. In this, fathers hold a unique responsibility. Not *sole* responsibility, mind you—because the mother quite often assumes the role of religious anchor in the black family unit—but a *unique* responsibility.

It is a role our fathers should cherish and one, unfortunately, that is often overlooked or unrecognized in the rush of today's hectic world. But it is one that will save and redirect our children's lives and strengthen the fabric of the black family unit. The old adage that "the family who prays together, stays together" is not merely a catchy jingle: it is miraculous in its intensity and accuracy.

Our Father is always there, always watching us, but too often we don't allow ourselves to actively, *mindfully* bask in His gaze. Too often we can't find the time to still ourselves long enough to simply revel in His heavenly presence. Particularly for children who are fatherless, absorbing this knowledge is paramount.

Fathers, teach your children this: that even in this rough-and-tumble world, they are never, ever alone. Teach them that, even after you yourself leave this earthly place, they will continue to be nurtured, buoyed, and protected by a Father who will never leave them or forsake them.

Another lesson for our children, most powerfully taught from fathers themselves: God is real. That He is infinite, eternal, accessible, and unchangeable in His being, wisdom, power, holiness, mercy, and love. What solace this source of knowledge can be—especially for those young African American children who have negative or nonexistent relationships with their biological fathers! To realize that they will never *really* be fatherless, that their Heavenly Father will be with them always. He is the constant. The beginning and the end. The Alpha and the Omega. Never absent. Never tardy or tentative in His grip or His grace.

The Soles of His Feet

My father, James W. Clark, was a prayerful man. Whenever I visualize him, which is often, I see in my mind's eye the soles of his feet, light tan in color, just about the shade of a cup of coffee into which someone has poured a little too much cream; smooth and leathery as well, like two small pieces of animal hide that are stretched and dried, then stretched snugly over the top of an African drum. When I think of him, I find myself conjuring up the vision of the soles of his feet with more clarity than I recall his handsome, chiseled face (and yes, it *was* a strikingly handsome face). It seems a strange thing to remember, my father's feet.

As a child, I'd occasionally glance through my parents' bedroom door, which was always kept slightly ajar. Daddy would often be kneeling at his bedside, head bent in silent prayer, his left foot slightly folded over the sole of his right, in a pensive, childlike, pigeon-toed fashion. On the floor beside him lay his blue bedroom slippers, waiting patiently at attention, like two terrycloth sentries, until he ended his prayer and rose slowly from his knees. As he rose, he'd sometimes reach to rearrange his slippers in a "just so" position, then crawl into bed. But most often—and to my great delight—he'd wiggle his right foot into one slipper, then his left foot into the other, so that he could make his way back throughout the house to kiss all seven of us good night. (By the time he pushed his foot into his right slipper and had commenced to wiggling into his left, I'd have long since scampered quietly to another bedroom or downstairs to the kitchen with Mother—expertly avoiding those creaking, popping places in our floorboards—lest he spy my intrigued, intruding eyes upon him during what I'm sure he considered the holiest, most private moment of his day.)

Some people say that the eyes are considered the "windows to the soul." Not so with me—particularly as I learned to look deeply inside my father's soul. No, it wasn't the eyes at all. God allowed me to see into Daddy's soul—and, hence, into His own Divine Soul—by allowing me those brief, beautiful glimpses of the soles of his feet.

Because of the position of my parents' bed, Daddy's back was always turned toward me when he knelt to pray, so I was never quite sure how he held his hands during prayer; whether they were clasped, folded, cupped, or palm to palm. But of this much I was certain: his hands were *touching*, judging by the position of his arms, bent at the elbow and tucked in closely against his sides. I was also equally certain of the fact that he made the sign of the cross every time he finished praying—such a familiar, faith-filled gesture to me even as a child that I could easily recognize it even from behind. I recognized it because it was Daddy who taught all seven of his children how to make the sign of the cross correctly when we were small. And when I saw it, I saw it not only with my eyes, but with my mind, body, and soul. The swift, graceful movement of his right upper arm—fingertips up to forehead, then straight down the chest, across to the left shoulder, then traversing the chest to touch the right shoulder. (When I make the sign of the cross even today, as a grown woman, I think *first,* of course, of Christ the King; but then I think of Daddy. I suppose I've come to see the sign itself as a vital, visible, deeply personal link between my Heavenly Father and my earthly father. How blessed I am to be a part of that everlasting, inextricable, living link! A woman raised her entire life within the loving embrace of not only one father, but *two!*)

My father was a peaceful, pensive man. It was always difficult to tell precisely what was on his mind—or moving in his heart—because he rarely allowed his facial expressions to betray his feelings. Aside from the occasionally clenched jaw or furrowed brow that would move across his face as quickly as a dark storm cloud when he was angry, Daddy's feelings were, for the most part, inwardly turned. His character showed itself primarily through his actions. He was full of faith; of that, everyone who knew him was certain. His spirit soared high and sang loudly: it arrived boldly into a room even before *he* actually did. I'm certain that he loved God more than he loved himself, more than he loved *us,* even—as it should be. By putting God first—above all else—above, even, the desperate, searing love he felt for his wife and seven children, he was filled to overflowing with God's grace, boundless and infinite; perhaps even a little beyond our (and his) human comprehension. Here was a man whose heart was filled with much, much more than an earthly, paternal love for his family. Dad purposefully opened his heart, mind, and soul to receive the love of his Heavenly Father—which was good not only for him.

It was good for us.

What we received was the benefit of the rippling effect: like a pebble being dropped in the center of a pond, we received steady, soothing ripples of paternal love. We were awash in it. Both earthly and heavenly.

What I loved about Daddy was how he allowed his godly spirit to lead him, and he was not a man who was embarrassed or timid about praying publicly. When I was a child, my perception of him was that he was in a constant state of prayer. I remember specific, sparkling prayerful moments: at my Aunt Bunny's bedside, for instance, when he picked me up from school and we went to visit and pray with her, or when Scottie, his best friend, took a nasty fall down his front stairs and hurt his leg. Yes, Daddy prayed for everything and everybody; probably for the sick and shut-in; for the sun, the moon, and the stars, and for the lilies of the valley that he tended to so lovingly in the grassy patch next to our back porch (which still bloom every year in that same spot, even today).

My spiritual memories of Dad remain vivid. Memories of the nine of us sitting around the kitchen table (Daddy at the head, Mother at the "other head"), giving thanks to the Lord, "for the food we are about to receive." At the kitchen table, my "high chair" consisted of two thick telephone books stacked on top of each other and draped with a yellow towel, my short brown legs dangling and swinging happily under a table crowded with sixteen other knees, legs, and feet. I'd pray right along with everyone else, my eyes squeezed tightly shut (as if, perhaps, the tighter they were shut, the better God could hear me). I had my own "toddler translation" of our dinner prayer: "For the nourishment of our bodies" became "for the moorishment of our bobbies." But whether I got the words exactly right was not important. What was important was that I was praying. And I was praying with my family. As we came to the end of prayer, all of us (except Mother) would peep out of one eye to steal a look at Daddy. The millisecond after he began to make the sign of the cross, we'd all follow in unison. Following Daddy's lead.

And *enjoying* being led.

Although I grew up in a house filled with the glorious presence of God, and we went to church regularly, it was the early image of Daddy's solemn bedside praying that had the most profound and lasting effect on me and that opened my own heart *and* my mind, in a deeply personal way, to the existence of God and the profound power of prayer. This man who was my father was larger than life; strong and stern, a man of few words. That he was able to still his soul and create a place of solitude and solace for the sole purpose of communicating directly with his Heavenly Father (a tall order, given that there were nine of us under one roof), touched me deeply. It was Daddy who taught me, through his actions and through the soles of his feet, that our Heavenly Father is *always* accessible, always eager to listen to our prayers. It was Daddy who showed me—who showed all of my siblings, really, right alongside Mother—that God is *not* an unapproachable, remote abstraction, but rather an absolute and unchanging spirit in this ever-changing, connect-the-dots, hyperkinetic world in which we live. And as if *that* breathtakingly bold and beautiful knowledge is not enough to burst one happily at his spiritual seams, here's the icing on the cake: God's eternal love for His children is not only real, but *free for the taking*—as freely as I'd swipe the very real apple from the very real fruit bowl on our very real kitchen table on my way outside to play hide-and-seek with my very best childhood friend and next-door neighbor, Cookie.

———◆———

Novelist Richard Wright remembers the childhood joy
he felt in church, with his family:

"Our going to church on Sunday is like placing one's
ear to another's chest to hear the unquenchable
murmur of the human heart."

———◆———

When I was a little girl, this knowledge of God was my *absolute* in a relative world. It helped me make sense of my daily life. To a child still learning to tie her own shoes, He was my source of comfort and confidence. To a preteen who could never quite figure out the silly things in life—like how Ginger managed to stay so glamorous in her shimmering, full-length gowns on that tiny desert island—He provided a way for me to distinguish between what is real (His glory) and what is not (that "stupid-head" Ginger wasn't stranded on an island at all, but cooped up in a tiny television studio filled with fake sand, bright lights, and plastic palm trees). And even though Gilligan's half-baked, wholly unsuccessful rescue plans were teeth-grindingly frustrating, my Lord had a way of making all the frustrations and perplexities of my young life—even the silly things— simply *fall away*, like leaves blowing off a tree.

I love my Daddy, and I love my Heavenly Father!

My point, of course, is that my father cared less than a whit about my perception of Ginger and Gilligan, even though their predicament seemed, at times and to me alone, moderately significant. What Daddy was concerned with was my understanding and appreciation of the glory of God. And to this day, I still smile inside when my children and I watch reruns of Gilligan and that shimmering "stupid-head" Ginger.

Yes, I am blessed and smiled upon in that my father and my mother loved me enough to raise me and teach me in the ways of the Lord. And what did He teach me? A note card I came across in a local bookstore says it best:

That "life is fragile; so handle with prayer."

God and Mr. Pike

Believe it or not, I still remember seeing the first freshly caught fish of my life. My father and I were on our front lawn, he kneeling in front of me, to proudly display a giant pike he'd just caught on a fishing trip.

*Even as a toddler in diapers I remember
thinking, "What a hero my dad is!"*

He knelt gently in toward me, showing me his prized catch, watching me closely to make sure I wouldn't be scared by the sight of a fish that was a little taller than I was. (I was also told by my sister that a few hours later, as the sun was setting on that same day, and purple and violet-colored streaks marked the sky, we all gathered around the kitchen table, blessed the food, and *ate* poor Mr. Pike for dinner. Mother, or one of my older sisters, reached over to my plate to carefully separate the fish from the bone so that I wouldn't choke on my small portion of old Mister. Looking back on it, Mr. Pike was the first fish I'd ever tasted. . . . Maybe that's why I love fresh seafood to this very day.)

Later that same evening, I saw Dad kneeling again, not on one knee this time, but on both, in his usual bedside-prayer position.

Reflecting on it now, decades later, I'd like to think that Daddy was asking God to watch over him and his entire family as we settled in for the night's slumber. Perhaps he was also praying for rain the next day (we'd been experiencing a drought) and world peace. But most of all, my educated guess is that he was saying a deeply felt prayer of thanks to God for the day's bountiful catch, and for being able to share with us—by *feeding* it to us—the fruits of his labor. I think I probably said a very little girl's prayer that evening myself, too; thanking God for Mr. Pike and all the joy (and "moorishment") that fish brought to our entire family that day.

In the end, Mr. Pike was an edible, temporary, culinary pleasure for all of us, and a great source of pride for Daddy. But old Mister vanished in a flash—as soon as we could lift our knives and forks. He was caught, shown off to the family, then eaten up. Gone forever. Mr. Pike's time on this Earth (and in the water) was short-lived. No so with God. We can consume His love ceaselessly, fill our hearts and minds constantly with His glory. What He gives us is something renewable and everlasting. It will never vanish. Unlike Mr. Pike, His goodness will live on and on and on.

"Forever" might be the better word.

Can I get an "Amen"?

Time to "Get Right" with God

When black fathers carry and nurture the love of God within themselves, that spiritual energy is bound to nudge and nestle itself into the hearts of their families. It *has* to, because His glory is complete and wonderfully contagious. If *all* fathers—black or white—fill themselves with His boundless love, it will be impossible for them to keep His grace and mercy a secret from those they love, particularly their children. Why would they want to? In this cruel, shortsighted world we live in today, it becomes even more important for fathers to step directly up to the plate and purposefully shower God's goodness over the entire fabric of their family structure, however that family structure may be configured. For black fathers who haven't been surrounded by the glory of God—historically, as a natural part of their upbringing—those first few steps up to the plate may be difficult to take alone.

For this reason, black pastors, religious leaders, and clergymen must hold themselves responsible and accountable for actively reaching out to black families and fathers (particularly single or widowed fathers) who are in need of a road map and a guiding hand as they begin their spiritual journey; a journey that must first begin within, then ripple outward to touch their families and children.

Getting right with God involves opening your heart to Him, quieting your soul so that you may hear Him speak. It requires time, mental discipline, and an eagerness for solitude. In this fast-paced, frenetic world, creating that spiritual space is often difficult and discouraging. Nobody has time. Everybody is busy. Black men especially are faced with tremendous daily juggling acts. Their inner voice whispers, "Stay on top of things on the job. Be in the mix. Make that deadline. Meet those projections. Watch your back. Watch your white counterpart. Watch your neighbor. Watch your friend." But there is another, more powerful voice that can be heard more clearly in the stillness and silence. It is the voice of God. But in order to hear it, one has to *make the time*—which means making the purposeful effort—if only for a few minutes in the morning and evening. Just as my father did and just as I do, create a quiet place to commune with God. And out of that stillness will come something powerful and profound.

Mother Teresa said: "Listen in silence, because if your heart is full of other things you cannot hear the voice of God."

What this means in contemporary society is that Palm Pilots, cell phones, fax machines, and laptops certainly have their place and function, but they serve as dangerous distractions when they disrupt our reflective personal and family time with God. What this also means is that, by stilling your soul to commune with the Heavenly Father—daily, regularly, and eagerly—your spiritual roots will begin to grow, enabling you to create a stronger foundation for you and your family, and face, head-on, life's daily struggles and demands, which will, somehow, become much less overwhelming.

———◆———

But more than my own words, listen to the wise words
of a man who was both a father and a Father:

"There is no argument needed for the necessity of taking time out for being alone, for withdrawal, for being quiet without and still within. The sheer physical necessity is urgent because the body and the entire nervous system cry out for the healing waters of silence. One could not begin the cultivation of the prayer life at a more practical point than deliberately to seek each day, and several times a day, a period when nothing happens that demands active participation. . . .

"At first the quiet times may be quite barren or merely a retreat from exhaustion. One has to get used to the stillness even after it has been achieved. The time may be used for taking stock, for examining one's life direction, one's plans, one's relations, and the like. This in itself is most profitable.

"It is like cleaning out the closets, or the desk drawers, and getting things in order."

—REVEREND HOWARD THURMAN,
MEDITATIONS OF THE HEART

There is much value in the notion—as Thurman says—of "cleaning out the closets" and "getting things in order" so that we might become better people and more faithful fathers (and mothers). Creating silence to feed our souls is a wonderful way to reflect on our character and bring God close in around us.

Yet another reflection from Mother Teresa:

Silence of our eyes.
Silence of our ears.
Silence of our mouths.
Silence of our minds.
. . . in the silence of the heart
God will speak.

Fathers: create that silence and it will change your life. It will give you peace. It will connect you directly with something infinitely larger than yourself. And when you reach out to touch your family, they, too, will feel its power.

The concept of "Getting Right with God" doesn't mean that you were ever "wrong" with Him. What it means is that we can *always* draw closer to Him—and by drawing closer into His presence, we create a tremendous spiritual force that bubbles within and touches everything we do. Prayer is a good way to "get right."

A man I met for this book, James Anthony Carter, is the father of four girls, and happily married. He is a spiritual "father-teacher" to his children. When he speaks, he glows.

"Prayer is an important part of my family life," he said to me recently as we smiled into our coffee. "When my family blesses the food, for instance, we do it collectively."

More glowing. The room becomes brighter.

"But the rule in our house is that when the collective prayer is finished, everyone gets to say their own, individual prayer. My daughter Atir [his wife's name, "Rita," spelled backward] can get a little *long-winded*."

A worried look flashes across his face as fast as lightning.

"I don't mean to be disrespectful," James says, looking up to the ceiling, as if apologizing. "But Atir can go on and on and on! She'll start with, 'I want to thank you, God, for the bus driver bringing me home safely so I can eat this good food that Ma has cooked. I want to thank you for this chicken I'm about to eat, and even though I don't like broccoli that much, I want to say thank you for that, too.' "

He smiles, proud father that he is.

"And then she'll thank the grocery-store bagger who helped load the food into the car and maybe ten or twenty other people or things. If we *let* her, she'd sit at that table and thank the whole world. Well, she prays until the food gets cold. And the second she's finished, everybody pushes back their chair and gets in line at the microwave to reheat their food."

I smile at the image, a familiar one in my own home, at our dinner table.

"But we let her go on and on, and we honor the entire process," Carter continues. "Because . . . because you can never take too much time—especially a little girl—when you're praying from your heart."

Atir, I'd say, is busy getting right with God.

Whether the prayer is energetic and enthusiastically long-winded, like Atir's, or in the solitude of silence that Mother Teresa so cherished, or even the bedside prayers that were my father's, the very act brings us closer to God.

Fathers of Faith: it's time to "Get Right."

As almost any brother pastor in America says during the invitation to discipleship, with his arms held high in a wide, welcoming embrace, "The doors of the church are now open."

Come, let's take this walk together. For your family; for your children. For yourself.

The doors to the church are now open.

The doors are open. . . .

Will you come?

◆

One eloquent passage captures it all:

"My father . . . believed that the mere act
of seeking the kingdom brought all things unto you."
—ADAM CLAYTON POWELL, JR.

◆

*I Don't Even Know My Own Father.
How, Then, Can I Know God?*

◆

"My Father in Heaven has guided my hand—
without ceasing—as I've raised every one of my children.
My kids look at me and see 'Dad.'
When they look heavenward, they see 'Father.' "
—VINCENT MATHEWS,
AUTHOR, PASTOR, AND CHILDREN'S ADVOCATE

◆

Black fathers who have negative, destructive, or nonexistent relationships with their children are not only copping out, but losing out. The children themselves are losing out, too—in more ways than one. But for the purposes of this specific chapter, let us focus on the child who knows nothing of either father, earthly or Heavenly.

I was guided toward a miracle of a man named Vincent Mathews, a married African American father who lives in Detroit, another spiritual "father-teacher," not only to his own seven children but to countless young people throughout the city. Talking with him, I was reminded of my own father, not only because Mathews is the father of seven children, just like Dad, but because he, too, is a "rippler," sending soft, spiritual waves undulating toward everyone he meets.

Author of *Freedom Journey: A Holistic Approach to Achieving Success in the 21st Century*, Mathews worries about young people, particularly African American males, who are fatherless or who *feel* fatherless. The paternal void can get in the way of how they come to view themselves as men, contributing to their inability to nurture strong, healthy relationships, earthly or spiritual.

But he has a solution.

"The bottom line is this," he says. "If I am to reflect God to my children, they have to see me as a source of strength, a source of comfort, of trust and stability; not just a man who helps pay the bills and keeps the food on the table. When the glory of God shines through *me*, it shines also

The family that prays together stays together

through to my children. I take that responsibility as a father very seriously."

His spirit spurs him on. The question he asks me is a good one:

"How can our African American children who are fatherless—biologically or psychologically—conceptualize God as a kind and loving Father when they can't even visualize their *own* fathers as kind and loving?"

The question gives me pause.

He continues, "If I had a dime for every young black male who has come through my door in absolute turmoil over his relationship with his father—or with the absence of a relationship with his father—I'd be a wealthy man. But that's not the kind of wealth I want."

"When they come to see me, they are in pain. I can see it in their eyes. It's almost a physical pain. They're angry and resentful. They feel like they've been tossed aside and thrown away. They're struggling with low or no self-esteem because they've been abandoned by their fathers, and they're so furious about it that they're blinded. What I try to do is help them open their eyes again, so that they can see clearly."

As I listen to Mathews describe these young people, I recognize, again, that theirs is a pain I have never known. It is a bitterness I have never tasted. I will never have to carry it somewhere in the deepest depths or even at the shallow surfaces of my soul, nor conceal it as a haunting part of my past. But what it also makes me realize is this: our desire to embrace and uplift those young black males (and females) who feel abandoned and embittered should be collective and deliberate. It must be active and self-propelled. Because the last thing they need is our pity. What they need is our support. Our love. The promise of our collective embrace.

"Even though many black fathers may not realize it," Mathews says, "many of their children are struggling and fighting to get past the negative, ugly images they have of their own fathers so that they can make it to that beautiful image of the Almighty God they hear me talking about."

Mathews's seven children know they are bountifully, doubly blessed with not only a solid and loving earthly father, but with a loving Heavenly Father as well. Therein lies a wellspring, for them, of faith and confidence. Of connectivity. His good work with black youth and black fathers is, no doubt, saving lives and strengthening spirits. But it's also making society at large aware of the fact that all young people need to be led by the hand and guided. Mathews helps us realize the fact that having a strong, faith-filled male figure in a young person's life is not just a "nice" thing to do to strengthen the fabric of black America, but mandatory if families are to remain strong. At this point in our history, with familial lines so tenuously and loosely connected, we are in dire need of the spiritual glue of which Mathews speaks to bind us together. Anything less spells certain doom for African American families. Do we want to see the traditional and historical spiritual fabric of the black family unravel at the seams even more than it already has?

Mathews's answer, and mine as well, is an emphatic "No!"

Search your heart and see if you agree.

When Father is close, there is peace. Shouldn't it stand to reason, then, that when we call Him into our presence, we will create an environment for ourselves and our children that, by definition, is pure and peaceful? Is what I describe so simple a concept that it becomes too complex for us to fathom? So beautiful in its power and simplicity that we are unable to actualize it? Is it too complex a task to teach ourselves to sit still—at least long enough to hear a Voice other than our own?

Here's an idea; a proposal if you want to call it that: let us listen closely—*all of us*—to the last verse of the Old Testament. In order to hear it, we must seek and find serenity in the midst of our daily, chaotic activity, a difficult discipline and a seemingly impossible task. But can you hear it? It is a call for fathers and their children to come together. It is a warning that, if we do not bring father and child together again, certain and specific harm will come to all of us.

◆

These are not my earthly, secular words, but the eternal
words which appear in the Holy Bible:

"And He shall turn the heart of the fathers to the children,
and the heart of the children to their fathers,
lest I come and smite the earth with a curse."
—MALACHI 4:6

◆

God is telling us to turn our hearts toward Him, *and* toward our children. If we are wise, we will listen.

I, for one, don't want the earth and all of its inhabitants to be smitten with a "curse." I want and need to place myself into a prayerful state and meditate on the words in Malachi, to pray for the prospect of fathers and children to love each other again. I don't need to be a man *or* a father to do that.

All I need to be is a concerned child of God.

———◆———

Carry these next few passages around with you, deep
in your heart, and share them with your family:

"Look to God as the author of your family life; count on Him to give you all that is needed to make it what it should be. Let His Father-heart and His Father-love be your confidence. As you know and trust Him, the assurance will grow that He is fitting you for making your home, in ever-increasing measure, the bright reflection of His own."

—ANDREW MURRAY,
AUTHOR OF *RAISING YOUR CHILDREN TO LOVE GOD*

———◆———

"Honor thy Father . . . that thy days may be long
upon the land which the lord thy God giveth thee."
—EXODUS 20:12

———◆———

3.

A MATTER OF PRIDE

STORIES FROM FATHERS
WHO REFUSE TO LOSE PRIDE

The spirit of this chapter is somewhat dimmed by the storm clouds of crisis and calamity. In it, I sit down with several African American fathers who have faced or are facing an uphill battle with their lives or their pasts, but whose proud paternal spirits blow those storm clouds away like a strong wind.

I celebrate these fathers who are struggling, but surviving. I hold them up in recognition because they realize, now, the mistakes and missteps they may have made as fathers and as men early on in their lives, but they have sought redemption and found—in the process—personal restoration.

For them, the sun is beginning to peek out from behind the clouds. Some of their words and personal reflections rumble like thunder threatening in the far-off distance. But their pride has a steadying effect; it calms the winds and stills the storms.

It is not by accident that I use the metaphors of stormy days and rumbling thunder when I introduce these men. On the day that I met and interviewed these fathers at the Center for Creative Non-Violence (one of the largest homeless shelters in Washington, D.C.), the skies were gray and the rain fell in fat dollops.

The moment I entered the shelter, I realized that the sun had hidden completely behind the clouds, in more ways than one. As the interviews progressed, however, even though the rain outside continued its dreary downpour, the spirit in the room began to brighten like the rising sun.

So as much as I want to celebrate all that is good about black fathers in this book, it is equally important for me to include, as a part of this celebration, a glimpse of those fathers who haven't always seen the sun; who have lost their way along the path of life but are struggling hard to regain a solid foothold during their uphill climb; who may still be wrestling with feelings of shame or inadequacy—as fathers *and* as men—because of their earlier, seemingly irrevocable mistakes.

The Scripture warns us often about resisting the temptation to judge our fellow men: *Judge not, lest ye be judged.* It is not our job to judge—but to examine, probe, uncover, uplift, and inspire. And what right is it of ours, being the imperfect beings we are, to judge another anyway? Have we not all committed grave, egregious errors in our lives that could have rocked our foundation to its very core? The difference is that most of us are lucky—blessed—to have escaped the consequences of our most serious errors. *Let he who is without sin cast the first stone.*

For fathers who may have stumbled along the way, know that you are still loved. For the men who hurt but are on the path to healing, know that you are not alone. We, all of us, need to be with them. God, we already know, is close around them. And their own personal pride is beginning to shine through once again. Even after the storm.

Getting Inside the Pride

"I've made mistakes. Did some bad things—whatever it took, in fact—to provide for my children and family. Messed myself up pretty bad. Wasn't always there for my kids like I should have been. I know all that. I've paid my dues, asked for and received forgiveness from my children—which took me a long time—and I'm living for today. Not yesterday. I'm proud of my children and I know with all my heart that, after all this time, they love me."

—JESSE MARTIN, FATHER

The constant noise jangled my nerves on a day when my nerves were already frayed at the edges: The police sirens just outside. The loud, scratchy intercom. The clanging of gates and slamming of doors. Someone hollering in the hall. A pair of eyes peering at me through the window of the wall.

There I was, in one of the largest homeless shelters in D.C., trying to make the sparse room they'd given me for my interview sessions feel "comfortable" or at least conducive to discussion. I had a desk, two metal folding chairs, a brown swivel chair missing one "swivel," and a Naugahyde sofa in the adjoining room that was just too heavy for me to try to drag into the interview area. My shoes and feet were wet from the rain, my spirit was soggy, and all I could see from the gated window that looked onto the street was rain and more rain. There wasn't much I could do to brighten up the room except say a silent prayer before my first interview arrived and take one last look around the room, my eyes resting on the swivel chair that sat leaning and hunched into itself like an old man with a bad back.

I decided on the metal folding chairs.

As it turned out, I needn't have given the arrangement of the room as much thought as I did.

When Mr. Jesse Martin walked in, he looked around the room momentarily, made his way to a folding chair, and sat down crisply. I got up and pushed the swivel-less chair into a far corner, not wanting to risk having someone sit on it and lose his balance. But Mr. Martin seemed more than balanced. Here was a man of both balance and dignity. He wore his pride like a halo all around him.

"Don't go rearranging the furniture all around," he said; not repri-manding me, really, but definitely sensing my jittery, jangled nerves. "I appreciate the effort, but I'm fine right here where I am. Really."

He began straightaway:

"They told me you wanted to hear me talk about my being a father," he said. He wasted no words, no movement. He looked me straight in the eyes, and I returned his gaze.

"I'm the father of eleven children," he launched in efficiently, arms folded in front of him. "Nine girls, two boys. Eighteen grands. Nine great-grands," he said, the beginnings of a smile forming at the center of his lips and spreading outward, softening his face. I regarded him, thinking that he didn't look old enough to have grandchildren, much less great-grands.

He regarded me regarding him.

He must have felt the need to explain: "My first child was born when I was fourteen years old. My eleventh child was born when I was fifty-four, just recently. So if you do the math, you'll see there's a forty-year differ-ence between my first child and my last."

My mind wouldn't let me do the math. The sound of distant thunder and splattering rain was distracting me, making me think of my own father.

Mr. Martin reached into his back pocket to pull something out. Against my will, I looked quickly toward the door, which a staffer had in-tentionally left wide open by fitting a rubber doorstop snugly underneath, "for security reasons," he'd said before leaving me alone in the room. The security desk was just outside—in clear vision as long as the door was left open.

These men were *homeless,* I reminded myself, not hardened *criminals.* I kicked myself mentally in the shins for my melodrama and prejudice. *Judge not.*

Finally, Mr. Martin fished out a worn, brown leather wallet from the back pocket of his pants. I sat where I was.

After retrieving it, he flipped it open easily with his right hand, hold-ing something out that he obviously wanted me to see. I leaned forward, peering closely: a wallet-size color photo of a beautiful brown girl with bright eyes and neat braids. She was missing a front tooth and hugging a thick tree trunk, a painted scene of an English countryside behind her. She looked to be about seven years old.

"That's my little girl," he said with pride.

His eyes danced against his will.

The photo seemed to break the ice and breathe warm air into the room. But the sirens continued blaring outside. The intercom kept crackling. More sets of eyes—and bodies—peered through the window, male residents of the shelter who merely wanted to see what was going on.

"If you ask me whether I think I've got good children, the answer is 'yes,' " he said, moving deeper into the subject of fatherhood quite on his own.

"But I'll tell you this, and I'm not apologizing for it—I'm only explaining it to you: being a black man and a father to eleven children has had its trials and tribulations."

"I didn't know my children when they were growing up as well as I would have liked to," he added frankly.

Outside, another police cruiser sped by, sirens wailing and tires splashing dirty water against the side of the building.

What stopped you from getting to know them?

"First of all, I served fifteen years in prison," he answered. "Most of my children were babies when I went in. And out of eleven children, eight of them had different mothers. It was very, very hard trying to keep a relationship going with them while I was on the inside."

He shook his head suddenly, as if a bee or a mosquito had flown into his face. His hands went quickly up to his ears.

"Sometimes I can't hear myself *think* in this place, with all this noise," he said, getting up as quick as lightning to remove the doorstop and slam the door shut.

This time, I allowed my heart the luxury of jumping just a beat or two. Because the heavy metal door had been slammed shut, my view of the security desk was completely obscured. No, it wasn't obscured; it had completely vanished. All I could see was a small crowd of men slowly gathering at the window in the wall. I glanced at the only other window in the room, which faced the street. Gated and padlocked. I glared down at the stupid, inert rubber doorstop lying askew in the corner of the room, cursing the company that made it and forcing myself to provide Mr. Martin with at least as much dignity as he was mustering for himself. The *timing* was just a bit off color: here he'd just told me that he'd spent fifteen years in prison, then in the next moment—because he "couldn't hear himself think"—he got up and created a thick privacy around us. I admit I was thrown a bit off balance; slightly scared, even—as anyone else would have been in a similar situation.

As it worked out, the modicum of privacy was precisely what we needed. We were just two people, talking. He was teaching me about fatherhood and sharing with me his experiences.

"I ended up in prison because I did what I had to do to provide for my family," he said without preamble or apology.

"I also knew I couldn't ever get no high-paying, high-level job in any corporation, and I had to do something quick for my family. Hell, I was *raised* in the streets, and I always knew if I was going to get anything, I'd have to get it myself. And in order to get it for myself, I'd have to take it from someone else. That's what I did when I was a kid, and it's all I knew to do when my family needed me," he said.

It wasn't for me to judge. I held my peace.

"Whatever I gave to my children—and I wanted to give them the best—meant I had to do something that was illegal," Mr. Martin said matter-of-factly. "What father wouldn't want the best for their kids? Providing for his children is something a father just *does*."

I couldn't judge him, but I could evaluate the things I was hearing. Otherwise, the session would have been useless. Here was a man, I thought, frustrated and paralyzed by the prejudice of an oppressive system, who wanted to do the right thing by his children. Still—and this is what I'd tell my own children—resorting to illegal activity can never be the solution. That he resorted to criminal behavior to provide for his children was not the answer—because what he was providing for them, he was taking from someone else; the breaking of not only a legal code, but a moral one.

"I did everything I could to beat the system, to provide for my kids, to make sure they had whatever they needed," he said. "Gamble, steal, drugs. . . . Years ago," he said, pointing to the rickety table that separated us, "if that table had been a store counter, I wouldn't have given a second thought to jumping right over it and stealing whatever I wanted or needed. I would have jumped across that table as if it were the most legal, the most normal thing in the world to do."

He tilted his head back slightly, remembering.

"Back then, my children were the sharpest kids on the block," he said with pride—misplaced pride this time, I remember thinking.

"I remember one of my daughters stayed sharp. I got her this full-length black leather coat and she was steppin' in style. I gave my children so much more than I had myself when I was a kid, which I guess is what every parent wants for their children, right?"

*"**Wrong**," my father whispered in my ear. Not if it's illegal.*

Mr. Martin didn't wait for my answer. His question must have been rhetorical.

"About two years ago," he said, sitting up straighter in his chair, "one of my sons was murdered right here on these city streets."

My heart lurched. I extended my condolence and sympathy, which he accepted with a curt nod of his head. This was the only time during my interview with Mr. Martin where pride and pity seemed to fit comfortably together.

"Somebody shot him to death because they wanted to bum a cigarette, and he didn't have one," Martin remembered.

"Granted, he was in the wrong place at the wrong time, but to *kill* someone because they didn't have a *cigarette*? "

He scoffed. Anger and grief grew thick in the air around us.

"What was my reaction?" he said, repeating my question. "At first I wanted revenge. I was mad as hell. But then, it began to dawn on me that I'd never see my son again. Just when I was getting to know him again after getting out of prison," he said with a dry, ironic smile.

A long pause.

"I saw my other son walking down the street a few days ago," Mr. Martin said.

"You know how you see someone coming toward you and you're about to say 'hello,' then you realize in a split second that they've already seen you and they weren't even *planning* to speak to you at all?"

I knew.

"Well, that's what my son did. He saw me and was about to walk right past me. But then at the last minute—he acted like he didn't even want to look up at me—he said, 'Hi, Jesse.' Just like that. He didn't even call me 'Dad.' He just said, 'Hi, Jesse,' as if it took so much out of him, just to acknowledge my presence. I said hi and kept on steppin'."

This, I imagine, hurt his pride more than anything. I felt his pain, not pitying him, just imagining the indignity and pain he must have suffered on the street that day, in front of his son.

Mr. Martin answered another of my questions, calmly and without malice or anger.

"I can't really blame him for being disappointed in me, maybe even a little embarrassed," he said. "I wasn't there for him when he needed me most. I was locked up. And while I was inside, he didn't try to communicate with me at all. It was only through 'sources' that I'd learned he'd graduated and was doing quite well for himself. I know he feels mad, and anger is still in his heart," Mr. Martin said unapologetically. "But you know what?"

I waited. Knowing the answer would come.

"I forgive him that," he finished. "I understand why he is angry. Hell, I was angry, too. At myself. At the world. At the unfair, racist world we live in. But now my heart is in a different place."

What moves a heart to a different place, and where has yours moved to?

"It's moved to a place of peace," he said simply.

"I no longer feel that hot hatred in my heart. The vengeance is gone. The bitterness has dried up and gone away. Even the guilt I used to feel about not being there for my children is just about gone, because I know that guilt doesn't really get me anywhere. It just keeps me hanging by my fingernails to the past. I'm ready to move into the future now."

Amen, Mr. Jesse Martin. Amen.

Guilt, hatred, bitterness, vengeance, and low self-esteem have no place in a heart that is ready to be turned around.

I allowed myself to smile.

"You look a little like one of my daughters when you smile like that," he said.

He'd caught me by surprise. I thought I was smiling to myself, on the inside. Looking back on it, I'm glad I let my smile show. We sat and smiled together for a moment, immersed in our own thoughts.

I wanted to hear him talk about getting past the bitterness. I wanted him to tell me about how he moved himself toward the light and, what's more, to hear him address the issue of asking forgiveness and redemption for his past sins.

He heard me thinking.

"Look, I know I am guilty of many, many terrible things," he said.

"But let me say this without sounding like I'm whining: I regret what I did and I'm sorry that I hurt people doing it, but I was doing all I knew *how* to do to provide for my kids."

Is there a larger picture, a final piece of the puzzle resting just beyond his grasp that he thinks he's close to finding that will help make sense of all of this?

"I've already found them," he said with a grin. "I've found the pieces.

"They can't bring my son back to life, and they certainly can't undo all the wrongs that have been done—but maybe they can give me the strength to keep turning my heart around and work harder at improving my relationship with my children."

"I see a bigger picture, all right," he said, shifting in his chair.

"The bigger picture is the systematic destruction of the black man in today's society."

He's been thinking this through carefully. I can feel it.

"Not only are we destroying each other, we're destroying our families and our communities," he said.

Here is another person I've spoken to who is sharing his uniquely personal experience as a father. *Destroying our families and our communities*—I let the words echo in my mind. He speaks from personal experience because he, too, has been there. Lived through it.

"To put it simply, Ms. Taylor, we're killing ourselves and our futures."

I sat quietly, listening.

"I know it's true because I lived it. I served time for it. My son died because of it. This system is set up to suck the pride right out of us," he says. "To make us feel bitter and frustrated to the point where we have nowhere else to look but down."

And finally, the black family. What will save us?

"We've got to get our pride back. Reach down, dust it off, and pick it right back up," he said matter-of-factly.

I smiled at the image, at his choice of words. *Reach down, dust it off, and pick it right back up.* His words only helped confirm what I knew all along: that the fabric of our families and the faith of our fathers may at times seem to be hanging on a thread, but it is still salvageable, still worthy of preservation and enormous pride. Therein lies reason to celebrate—and to work hard to attain this collective goal.

"Believe it or not, I feel like I've evolved," he said. "My pain and bitterness didn't just disappear magically by itself. I pushed it out of my life. Today, I've been given the responsibility of dealing with the elderly and the disabled here at the shelter," he added with pride.

"We've got guys who are seventy years old, guys who are handicapped, too—lots of them in wheelchairs. We may have all walked different paths. We may have lived lives that we're certainly not proud of," he said, building to a momentum, almost like a preacher, "but we have a common ground, and we're working together from that common place. We're working from a place that used to be full of bitterness and embarrassment but that is finally beginning to shine."

A sudden change of direction in the conversation:

"Don't misunderstand," he said as if to correct the impressions that may have been forming in my mind, "I'm not talking about heaven or anything like that, I'm talking about today. About here and now. About all the things we have left that we can do and all the things we have to leave behind if we are going to survive."

"I'm sorry it's raining outside, Ms. Taylor," he said apologetically.

An odd apology, because he himself had absolutely no control over God's plan to open up the skies.

"If the sun was shining, then I could explain to you better what I mean about a brighter day. And in the end, I do believe that all of my children love me, even the one who was about to walk right past me on the street."

And he added, almost as an afterthought, a sentence that made my heart wince:

"They all love me. Especially the one who was killed."

Mr. Martin rose from his chair. I rose with him. He reached for my hand and shook it, a firm, dignified pump.

"Put down there in that book of yours that I love my children more than anything else in the world," he instructed me.

"But the guilt, for the most part, is gone."

He turned away from me, then turned back, as if in afterthought, and gave me a quick hug.

Mr. Jesse Martin. The father of eleven children. Eighteen grands. Nine great-grandchildren. A man of immeasurable pride, trying valiantly to re-build his life in the world of today and now.

For him, yesterday is gone. And only a brighter future lies ahead.

After Mr. Martin's departure, I walked to the window and gazed outside at the rainy city streets, waiting for my next interview to arrive.

I walked outside the room toward the security booth. The staffer buzzed a loud buzzer that opened the steel gate into the security office and let me in.

"How's it going so far?" he asked.

His small office has a panel of several screens that monitor the comings and goings of the residents. A space heater glowed orange-red under his desk. He had the *Washington Post* opened, turned to the sports section.

"You have everything you need?" he asked helpfully. I say a silent prayer of thanks to the entire staff at the shelter. So willing and ready to help. Without realizing it, my eyes rested on a somewhat comfortable-looking armchair with all of its rollers intact, wondering if he'd let me borrow it momentarily—just long enough to roll it across the hall so that my next interviewee would be a bit more comfortable. I decided against it. The metal chairs would have to do.

Back inside my "office," I rearranged the metal chairs yet again. I'd rather sit side by side with my next interviewee, a man named Mr. Robert Deal, than behind the table. The table might separate us and our ability to communicate.

Again, I needn't have worried about the furniture arrangements at all. As I was fiddling with the blasted metal chairs, I heard a slight humming behind me; not a human hum, like my mother used to hum me to sleep at night, but the hum of an electrical apparatus.

I turned toward the door.

Mr. Deal was already inside, maneuvering his wheelchair expertly around my silly metal chairs. He looked up at me with a gentle smile. I avoided looking at the entire image of him in his wheelchair, focusing instead on his bearded, young face and my prepared line of questioning. We exchanged introductions and pleasantries, then began the business of focusing on fatherhood.

"Well, you can see I'm in this wheelchair," he said, fidgeting slowly, like hospital patients wriggle weakly in their beds trying to find a more comfortable position. I wondered if he was in any pain.

"And I've been in it since I was twenty-one, when my kids were pretty small."

He looked to be in his early to mid-fifties. He was reading my mind.

"That's a long time to be in a wheelchair," he said darkly.

What had happened, and how had it affected his ability to be a good father to his children?

He answered with a question.

"Can you imagine being stabbed and paralyzed when you're just twenty-one years old, when your life has only really just begun?"

He unfolded his story neatly, just as he might unfold a blanket he was preparing to place over his knees to warm himself on a blustery fall afternoon, maybe before a football game.

"Before it happened, I was the best football player around," he said with a shy, proud smile. (I kick myself now for forgetting to ask which position he liked to play. I would have liked to have known, and I'm certain he would have found a degree of pride and pleasure in being able to tell me.)

"After it happened, I felt like my life was over. I was blinded by anger; completely overcome, if you know what I mean."

I tried to imagine, but I couldn't. As hard as I tried, I just couldn't fathom his experience.

"Football was out forever. Walking to the store was out. And when it came to trying to be a good father to my children, well, that just wasn't happening, either."

He looked at me for a moment, then cast his gaze downward, suddenly overly interested in the brown-speckled linoleum floor.

Momentary silence.

"How could I even toss a ball around the yard with my children?" he asked, arms outstretched in futility.

"I was so messed up, so angry at myself for not being able to be the father I thought—no, the father that I *knew* I needed to be for my children—that I got strung out. I wasn't even a whole *man* anymore, much less an adequate father. Couldn't even get my ass up out of a chair. I'm not ashamed to admit it. It was too much for me to handle."

His honesty and openness breathed fresh air into the room. They seemed to make me sit up straighter, as if at full military attention.

"About three months after my injury, I got on drugs. The drugs got on me. We got on each other," he said. "And I felt completely covered up.

"I've been clean for about six years, but I did drugs constantly right up until then," he said, looking into my face.

His wheelchair whirred and hummed again, then sighed and seemed to deflate a little, as if its tires were as weighted by the pressures of life as he.

"That's a long time to be on drugs," he said.

"After a while, my kids' mother decided it just wasn't going to work anymore, which made things even worse. I was at the end of my life. My world was ending."

Where are your children now, and what kind of a relationship do you have with them?

"My two children are grown," he answered. "And I am so proud of both of them! My daughter just gave me another grandchild. She brought him down here just before Christmas. He's going to be a real knockout with the ladies," he said with a sly smile.

"Yep, I have one boy, and one girl. Or one man, and one grown woman, I should say."

We smiled together. I told him that I, too, had a boy and a girl.

"You're blessed, you know," he said.

I do know. I thank God every day for my healthy, happy children. I thank Him even when I'm not thinking about it. I thank Him even when my spirit is sagging and my days are dark.

"As far as my relationship with my kids," he began, idly fingering a chrome joystick bauble on the right arm of his wheelchair, "they know what the deal is. They know I'm struggling a little, but that I'm better now than I was a few years ago."

Another smile. More hope. No pity. More pride.

"My daughter knows that this shelter is a part of my life. So does my son, although I don't see him very often at all. The last time my son was here, I think it finally dawned on him that I wasn't the same person I used to be when he was a little boy. I think he finally realized that I am trying to *change,* which means a lot to me."

Change. How? Why?

"Well, for one, I should have tried to be a better father to my children, but I was struggling with my own demons when they were young," he says. "I think about it all the time. Every day I feel guilty about not having been there for them when they needed me most.

"But the way I see it now is that, even though I feel guilty, it won't be the guilt or the pain or even their anger that finally makes things better. It will be *me,* and how I look at myself and my future," he finished.

The chair sighed again, and Robert Deal seemed to sigh with it. I resisted the urge to take a quick peek at the tires of his wheelchair. Surely they must operate by hydraulics, filling and emptying themselves of air based on his relative weight shifts and balances. When he slumped, the tires seemed to audibly exhale.

"I also realize that there's no making up what has already been lost between me and my children," he said.

"How you gonna make up for thirty years of not being there?" he asked the linoleum floor.

He shifted a little.

"The only thing I can do *now*, I realize, is to show them that I'm a better person than I used to be."

Another redemption story.

The rain stopped.

Two blessings in a row from the Heavenly Father, I think to myself. Two fathers who have moved or are trying to move beyond their past fatherhood faults and step into the light of a new day.

"What has happened in my life and in my heart to make me believe that I'm a better person?" he asks, repeating my question and giving himself a moment to think.

"Being in this place, for one," he answered.

"Coming to this shelter was the best thing that could have ever happened to me."

"Why? Because it turned my life around, simple as that. When I came here, I was still on drugs. I didn't give a damn about anything."

I wondered how it felt. Not giving a damn about anything in the world. But this was a question I would keep to myself.

"This shelter has brought meaning to my life," he said, looking around.

A group of his friends have gathered just outside the open door. One of them waved. He waved back proudly, with a slight air of importance and, if I saw it correctly, a quick "thumbs-up."

"Shortly after I got here, I met a man who happened to be working on the handicapped floor at the time, on my floor," he explained.

"He pulled me into his office one day and asked me what the deal was with me. He asked me whether I realized I was destroying my life, and he asked whether I had any children. I told him I had two, then he told me that I'd better get myself back together—if not for my sake, then damned sure for theirs.

"I thought a lot about what he said after that," Mr. Deal remembered.

"In fact, that was a turning point for me. Having someone I didn't even know pull me aside and knock some sense into my drugged-up head made all the difference in the world."

This one man had turned another's life completely around with just a few powerful but thought-provoking words.

Both my Heavenly Father and the spirit of my earthly father whispered closely into my mind and my ear: "You never know how something you say or do will affect another person's life."

"That's when I started trying to turn myself around," he said. "Ever since he talked to me that day, I've been clean. No drugs. No alcohol. And now that my head is clear, I realize now that I have to give full and total credit to their mother."

Remorse. Pride. Renewal. Being large enough to give proper and full credit to his wife for raising their children in his absence, playing the dual (and impossible) roles of both mother and father—and having the courage to admit he'd do it all differently if he had the chance again.

He said of his wife: "Through it all, she *never* bad-mouthed me to the kids, not even when I was strung out. She never said a negative word about me, even though she easily could have. I'll always appreciate that in her. Because she helped the kids realize that I wasn't the terrible father that they were beginning to think I was when they were young. Black fathers need to give more credit to their wives and partners."

He smiled when I nodded in agreement.

"When the chips are down, if a husband and wife can stay together through the storm, it helps the entire family. It keeps them strong. 'Cause when a member of the family is on drugs—like I was—it's like the entire family is on drugs, because every family member has to suffer in their own way. The withdrawal. The mood swings. The desperation. The vicious cycle. My wife and my friend here in the shelter—the one who probably saved my life—are the ones who helped me through this ordeal.

"And now I'm getting myself back on track."

Mr. Robert Deal.

Mustering all of his pride and power to leapfrog over—even in his wheelchair—the guilt and pain with every ounce of strength he has in his heart. He, too, sees the promise of tomorrow.

Another voice sings the soulful song of hope and redemption. In her own words, poet Helen Steiner Rice lifts her voice to celebrate the sheer and deliberate will to "live a little better" and "add a little 'sunshine' " to our days:

"NEW BEGINNINGS"

How often we wish for another chance
To make a fresh beginning,
A chance to blot out our mistakes
And change failure into winning—
And it does not take a new year
To make a brand-new start,
It only takes the deep desire
To try with all our heart
To live a little better
And to always be forgiving
And to add a little "sunshine"
To the world in which we're living—
So never give up in despair
And think that you are through,
For there's always a tomorrow
And a chance to start anew.
—HELEN STEINER RICE,
FROM *EVERYONE NEEDS SOMEONE*

A new tomorrow, however, had nothing to do with the precise sequence of events as they unfolded that day at the shelter. Inside the shelter, the "sunshine" Rice writes about seemed to be trying to show itself. The "tomorrow" she speaks of was unfolding at that very minute. For the moment, the thunderstorm had ceased.

Just for the Moment

By the time Mr. John Prather entered the room, the rain had begun again. He, too, came in a wheelchair.

Lost lives. Lost limbs. But in their case, certainly not lost hope.

He began by talking about his parents.

"I'm one of eight children," he said, closing his eyes even at the outset of the interview.

Either he's on medication that makes him sleepy or the drowsiness is a symptom of his physical disability. He seemed, almost, to be asleep.

"My mother and father loved me very much, and we had a pretty close relationship. The only thing about my father . . ." he said, drifting off. I resisted the urge to jostle his arm to wake him up. I could tell he was struggling to stay with his thoughts, perhaps struggling even to stay awake.

"The only thing about my father," he tried again, "was that it seemed like he was never really *home*." The realization, spoken aloud, seemed to have shocked him. His eyes opened wider now, searching—and finding—my gaze.

"My father *tried* to be a good man. I remember him being a busy man. He worked very hard to provide for his family, but when he was home, he was always tired. Plus, he liked to do his share of drinking and gambling, if you know what I mean."

Mr. Prather was describing not only his own father, but thousands of other fathers out there who work so hard and so long to provide for their families that they have nothing left to give when they actually arrive home. A classic catch-22 if there ever was one: playing the dual roles of provider and nurturer simultaneously.

Mr. Prather looked down at his black Nikes. I thought he might have fallen asleep, but he moved a leather-gloved hand to readjust a knob on the lower part of his wheelchair.

"If you're writing about fathers," he said slowly, "write that I, John Prather, am the proud father of two beautiful daughters who love me very much. We are very, very close."

I told him that I would. Daughters should always love their fathers. *Isn't that the way it **should** be?*

Prather regarded me closely, as if seeing me for the first time since he entered the room.

"You and I look like we're about the same age," he said with a smile.

"No, Ms. Kristin, I take that back. You're a very pretty woman, and I'd bet you my last dollar that you're much younger than me."

A charmer. When I asked him how old he was, I told him he was just about right: we were, roughly, about the same age. But he seemed to be struggling with something unseen, his defenses up like a cement wall around him. I could see his pride trying to surface as well, but I somehow felt he was wearing most of it on his sleeve. Maybe the fact that we were about the same age made him feel slightly off balance, defensive. It was not for me to judge.

He went on to set the record straight: "Please understand that I'm only in this shelter temporarily," he said.

"Just for the moment," he added with confidence.

"I had to move out of my apartment because it was a putrid, stinking mess," he explained in a hard, angry voice.

"The situation was unbearable. Sweltering in the summer. Freezing in the winter. The grounds were filthy. Because of my being in a wheelchair, I lived on the first floor."

"The water pipes were always breaking, flooding my apartment constantly. I mean, it was as bad as it could have been. It was worse than bad. So I finally said, 'forget it,' and just left. That's how I ended up here."

"The management of that apartment complex knew exactly what they were doing," he went on, answering my next question. "They refused to invest *any* money in their shabby properties, deciding instead to spruce up the properties that were already pretty."

No judgments. Just a temptation to offer a bit of legal advice about how the gross negligence of his landlords might certainly be considered an ac-

tionable offense. After all, a man can't live in an apartment—much less maneuver in a wheelchair—when there's three inches of water on the floor every time a hard rain falls.

"I know I haven't been the perfect father, because there is no such thing. But I do feel, sometimes, like I was inadequate to them when they were younger."

A police cruiser slid slowly by outside. I hoped that D.C.'s finest were saving lives or catching drug dealers, not just cruising through the streets of the nation's capital, searching for jaywalkers or expired parking meters.

"I wasn't always there for my daughters," he continued. "Sometimes I just *couldn't* be, simple as that."

Simple, I think, but probably irreversible in his daughters' childhood memories, still lingering in their minds, even if they are forgiving minds.

I asked him to speak to the bigger picture of black men and black fathers; bigger, even, than his own personal circumstances. He was certainly up to the task, and full of advice:

"To brothers who are about to become fathers or who are thinking about becoming fathers, I would say this: stay right beside your woman and the two of you learn as much as you can about parenthood together, *before* you have kids.

"Educate yourselves about family planning. Get out there and learn something about it! Because the answers won't come to you after the kids have been born and you're struggling through life trying to make it. It just doesn't work that way."

"Also, brothers, *keep working and stay close by your woman while she's pregnant.*"

Another solid piece of advice. I was scribbling notes now, which seemed to empower him.

"Fathers and mothers need to try to stay together, through thick and thin," he said. "If not for their own good, then for the good of their children."

Prather seemed to be transforming himself before my very eyes. His advice continued.

"And to the mothers out there: learn how to accept the two words from your man that are sometimes the hardest words for him to say: 'I'm sorry.'

"Messing up is bad enough. Losing time with your children is even worse. But saying 'I'm sorry' and admitting your past mistakes only to have it thrown back in your face is about the worse thing you can do," he said.

In a sense, I agree. From my uniquely female perspective it has been my experience, throughout the years, that the five most difficult words a brother can ever force himself to utter are "I love you" and "I'm sorry." They are words that do not come easily for most men.

Mr. Prather turned out to be a gracious man.

After the interview, he waited for me to gather my things and he made a grand, sweeping gesture with his right arm, allowing me to exit through the door before him. An ambulance had stopped in front of the shelter. Two paramedics rushed in, heading upstairs with a gurney. Prather lingered in the hallway while I was admitted back into the security area to say my "thank yous" to the staff who had helped coordinate the day. When I came out, he was waiting for me there in his wheelchair.

"Your chariot awaits you, Ms. Kristin," he said with dramatic splendor, either happy that our conversation went so well or happier still that I was about to leave. (I choose to believe it was the former.)

I pulled on my trench coat, Mr. Prather helping me with my left sleeve from his wheelchair. Tugging at the Velcro that bound my black mini-umbrella, I turned toward the exit, ready to face the elements. He rolled his chair alongside me.

It was clear that he planned on escorting me outside.

"You're not coming out in all this rain, are you?" I asked, worrying about his health and how he would get himself dry.

"Of *course* I am!" he said, again with a dramatic flourish. "I must make sure you get safely on your way."

A true gentlemen. I suddenly had the distinct feeling that if I returned to the shelter next week, he would have checked out. He'd be gone.

Outside, Mr. Prather unraveled a roll-out hood from the back of his black nylon slicker. I opened my umbrella, trying to shield both of us from the rain.

"Goodbye, Ms. Kristin," he said, holding out his gloved hand, which I held and shook. It seemed a sad handshake. Or maybe it was just me who felt suddenly sad.

"Goodbye, Mr. Prather, and thank you," I said, turning to button my coat.

He sat there in his wheelchair in the gray drizzle, watching me as I made my way down the street.

When I looked back, he waved. A happy wave. Instinctively, I turned around and half ran through the puddles in the street, back toward Mr. Prather.

I handed him my umbrella. "Keep this umbrella if you're going to be outside today," I said.

He looked up at me quizzically and started to refuse it, but I handed it to him so quickly that all he could do was accept it.

Now I was walking-running to reach my car and escape the rain. I looked back once more, and there Prather sat in his wheelchair, my black umbrella in one hand, his other hand waving more of a "get going" than a "goodbye."

No matter their condition or their station in life, fathers define their measure of manhood, in a very real sense, based upon their ability to provide for their families. It is in our blood to be resourceful; to drain the very last drop of every ounce of grit and determination that exists within us to keep our families afloat and safe from turbulent seas.

We cannot and must not forget to celebrate the undying pride of our fathers, even—no, *especially*—those who are struggling. Whether they're homeless, hurting, or Hollywood stars, the pride rings true in their every word.

———◆———

An eloquent example:

"Of all my father's teachings, the most enduring was the one about the true measure of a man. That true measure was how well he provided for his children, and it stuck with me as if it were etched in my brain. I didn't know where I going next, but I knew failure wasn't an option."

—SIDNEY POITIER,

THE MEASURE OF A MAN

◆

So even those fathers who linger in the darkness, must, too, be recognized. They need not languish in the shadows alone. The definition of a functional family unit lies in the fact that every member surrounds its struggling member with a firewall of support. And in turn, the father, through good times as well as bad, is able to hold his head up in dignity and pride as he seeks, and sometimes struggles, to be a faithful father.

In closing this chapter, it was my Lord who took me by the hand and guided me directly down the aisle of a local bookstore to find this passage, which I share with joy, jubilation, and triumph—because *triumph over obstacles* is what this chapter is all about.

The Magic Shoe Man

◆

"With ten children to feed, shelter and clothe, my daddy always had to be doing odd jobs to make a few dollars. . . . His side occupation was fixing shoes. . . . The shoes he brought home to fix were always old and tattered, with holes worn in the soles. I used to think that my Daddy was a magician to repair those shoes.

"With his special leather cutting knife, he cut out the soles and heels to the exact sizes, then tacked them in place by using hundreds of tacks in perfect rows. He finished each shoe by hand-sanding the leather edges until they were smooth as new leather.

"Finally, he put shoe polish on those dirty, greasy worn shoe tops and brushed them until they were smooth as new leather and some semblance of a shine appeared.

"After three hours of work on these shoes, he took them to the owner and collected enough, maybe $1.50 a pair. This money could buy some work gloves to protect his hands from the searing heat, or some rubbing alcohol or liniment to soothe his aching arms, legs, feet or back. Or the money would be used for food and utilities—and usually was."

—JOSEPH W. SCOTT,
FROM *MAKING A WAY OUT OF NO WAY*

───◆───

To those fathers who struggle to enrich their lives, to increase their faith in themselves as fathers, and to maintain their dignity: keep fighting the fight. As you read the pages of this book, know that these shared stories and messages of encouragement are for you.

4.

FINDING THE FRIENDSHIP
IN FATHERHOOD

HOW HAND-HOLDING, BEAR HUGS, AND WARM EMBRACES ALLOW US TO LOVE OUR CHILDREN TENDERLY

I was on a plane recently and overheard a conversation in the two seats behind me that made my soul smile. A father and his young son, traveling together on vacation, were talking. Simply talking. The son asked his father, "What will we do when we get there, Dad?" his voice full of excitement. The father's response: "Let's decide together. We could walk along the beach, go boating, drink those frozen fruity drinks you like until our stomachs hurt, or maybe get some snorkeling in."

And then he lowered his voice and whispered into his son's ear: "I love you more than anything in the world, kid. You have become my best friend and traveling buddy. What would I do without you?"

There was a brief silence. I wanted to peek behind me, but I imagined they must be embracing.

This chapter celebrates not only the beauty of, but the necessity for friendship between a father and his children. This particular father and son had obviously traveled together many times before; they had established a comfortable rhythm with each other, the rhythm of friendship—along with the rhythm of respect that a child should show toward his father, and vice versa.

In our daily lives, and throughout our history, the black male has had to posture himself, at every turn, with his fists up, protecting himself and his family from harm or hatred. There has not been much room in his life for friendship and fun, especially when he's trying hard to raise a family, move up the career ladder, and worry about the bills, the bank account, and the boys who just moved in next door and look like troublemakers.

Friendship is important not only for the warm and fuzzy fun of it all, but for vital, long-term social reasons as well. A father who befriends his child is also instilling in that child an enhanced sense of self and a strengthened ability to nurture healthy, balanced relationships with others later in life.

For fathers, there is a delicate balance to achieve with their children; a fine tightrope to walk as they try to play the traditional role of both authoritarian-disciplinarian *and* nurturer, confidant, and friend.

But it is a tightrope that can indeed be traversed; and, with practice, traversed with skill and grace. It *is* possible—mandatory, I believe—for a man to be both father and friend to his child.

This chapter is a celebration of those fathers who play that dual, challenging role. To all of you father-friends, praise and applause.

◆

"On this day I will mend a quarrel,
search for a forgotten friend,
fight for a principle,
show gratitude to God,
and tell someone, 'I love you.' "
—QUINCY JONES

◆

Although I didn't realize it when I was little, my father was one of my closest and most faithful friends. Through the eyes of my youth, I saw him as a gentle giant; a handsome man with gleaming hair and a forearm strong enough to hold a two-and-a-half-foot pike by his gills just so I could get a look at the great fish that was taller than I was. It didn't dawn on me until now that his masterful bravado was a very real part of who he was; but so was the softness and safety of the friendship that he silently showered over every one of his seven children.

Fathers, back then, were the breadwinners. The pillars. The providers. Providers were too busy *providing* to take time to create and nurture warm friendships with their children. It just wasn't what providers did. Pillars didn't usually take time out to play a game of checkers at the end of the day with their children because they just didn't have the time or the energy. Pillars didn't take their families on picnics to Belle Isle or downtown to see the fireworks, even if it sometimes meant going on a weekday. Pillars didn't build their daughters a real-life playhouse in the backyard, with real glass windows and a roof with real tile. Pillars just didn't *do* that.

But my pillar did.

He built me a playhouse and loved his wife, my mother, in a way I've never seen a man love a woman. This is one of the many reasons why I loved Daddy so; because he loved Mother enough to let her know that he was always there for her, and he gave her the support and the sustenance she needed to fulfill her dreams. I loved him because I saw the way he cherished and respected Mother: unconditionally and without restraint, playing the role of supportive spouse and nurturing father not only because he loved *us*, but because he loved Mother enough to

Surrounded by his large, loving family, my father liked to keep all of us close around him. Here I'm pictured standing in front of him, his hands resting protectively on my shoulders

want to reach out and offer her the balancing pole she needed as she walked the tightrope that was her life.

By nurturing and supporting *us*, he was doing the same for Mother. He allowed her to pursue every dream she ever had. Not only did he allow the strategic, deliberate pursuit of her dreams—but he *facilitated* and *encouraged* her pursuit as well. They were partners in life, for life.

It is often difficult for black fathers today to play these dual, simultaneous roles: the "I run a tight ship" traditional role of stable pillar as well as the role of nurturer-friend. But take it from someone who knows: it is infinitely healthier for every family member (and I do mean every one) to not only allow but also to encourage the father to play these dual roles whenever possible.

When Daddy wore "both hats"—the hat that allowed him to befriend us as well as the hat that reminded the family that he was the stabilizing force and head of his family—it reaffirmed in our eyes the flexibility of his character and the boundless love in his heart for us, as well as for this ex-

A day in the sun, father and son

traordinary woman who was his wife. It also allowed him to form unique, distinctive relationships with each one of us.

This, too—the ability of a black father to develop healthy relationships with his children that exist independently of the mother—is a vital key we can use to unlock the secrets to successful father-child relationships.

Again, this is a truth that has only recently "bubbled up" to the surface of my collective conscience. These "truth bubbles" began rising recently, as I found myself spending hours with my siblings, asking

them to remember the unique relationships they shared with Daddy.
Over time, as my conversations with
my siblings became more pointed in
preparation for this book, a common
denominator began to emerge; one
that I certainly would not have stumbled upon unless I had been guided
toward it. It was the result of my conversations with my siblings that
gradually revealed the entirety of the
miracle that was Daddy:

His individual efforts to form
strong father-child bonds with each
one of us revealed a collective truth
about Daddy that is both moving
and mysterious: moving because his
efforts at relationship-building with
his children were so very quiet; mys-

Still hand-holding at the end of the day

terious because I had never even realized—until now, really—that Daddy
actually had a plan, now revealed through careful examination, that would
draw each of us closer to him in love and friendship.

With an engineer's skill and beautifully balanced precision, Daddy designed his own "paternal plan," customized it for each one of us, and created the tool with which to implement it. It was the focused attention he
gave to his plan that made us think—no, forced us to realize, after all these
many decades—that his relationship with each one of us was special and
unique.

The "tool" he used to implement his plan turned out to be the same
for each one of us, one that brought him untold hours of joy and personal
contentment, which he so selflessly shared with us. It was a tool composed
of two parts.

What was this mysterious tool my father used to create such loving, lasting bonds between himself and his children? Here is the tool my father used:

A rod and a reel.

Gone Fishin'

I've heard it said that fishing breeds friendships. No truer words were ever spoken, especially as these words related to my dad and his children. Daddy loved us enough to share with us his passion for fishing—and to reel us in closer to his heart and his life. Long before the phrase "quality time" came onto anybody's radar screen, Daddy had packaged it, lived it, and lovingly showered it over each of his seven children.

It wasn't until I spoke with my siblings to remember Daddy for this book that I realized the power of Daddy's rod and reel; the power, if you will, of his preconceived paternal plan: when I asked my siblings to reflect on which childhood experiences with Daddy burned most brightly in their hearts, their answers opened up my soul. One after the other, their individual memories revealed a collective plan that was really Daddy's all along. Their shared memories helped paint the portrait of the man who was much more than our father.

He was our father-friend; the magic man with the rod and the reel. And as we would leave the house on our water excursions, we'd happily hang out our symbolic sign for the rest of the world to see, in big, bold letters: **GONE FISHIN'**

Water Stories

My sister Tanya: "What I remember most tenderly about Daddy were the quiet moments we'd spend together on the water.

"Most times we'd drive to Canada, which, as a little girl, I thought was absolutely the most wonderful thing in the world," she says with a smile in her voice. "Imagine! Going to another country with just you and your father, sitting in the front seat, the car windows open and the wind blowing every little thing in the car all around—just to go fishing!"

Never mind that Canada was just a few miles away from our home in Detroit. She was right: in her eyes, her father was taking her on the journey of a lifetime; escaping with his daughter, if only for a few hours, to another country and another world filled with peace and fellowship. A pure and simple fellowship, between a father and his daughter.

And then, my sister gave me a gift, a memory that connected my past to my future in an inextricably powerful way.

Tanya remembered Mr. Pike, the giant fish Daddy caught and displayed so proudly on our front lawn when I was a mere toddler in diapers! The same fish we ate with such relish that evening for dinner. The fish that bolstered Daddy's pride in such a magnificent way.

As it turns out, she was with Daddy at the very moment he reeled in Mr. Pike more than forty years ago.

"I remember how Dad struggled so hard to reel that fish in," she says.

"I cried because it took him so long to get the hook out of that fish's mouth. I thought that fish was going to rear back and slap Dad with his fin, or pull him into the water and I'd never see him again."

A horrible thought. A world without Daddy.

She continues: "While you were looking at that fish on the front lawn in your diaper, I remember someone taking a picture. Your face had such a mixture of wonder and awe! And you knew [the fish] wouldn't hurt you because Daddy was there to keep you safe.

"Even today," she goes on, "being on the water reminds me of Daddy. Fishing was the magic that helped create the friendship between us. Every time I'm on the water, I think of him."

Like my sister, I am warmed by the water memories with Daddy. I think of the fishing trips he and I used to take together, the two of us dropping our lines into the murky, mysterious water in the twilight hours of the morning. With Tanya, Dad fished mostly from a dock. But Dad and I would fish from his gray aluminum rowboat; it was light enough to tie to the roof of our station wagon (which we did, with a few pieces of thick twine). On the water, in between bites of cheese sandwich, which Daddy had prepared, I'd keep my eyes open for a pull on the line and my ears open for the promising tinkling of the tiny copper bell at the end of the pole.

Ours was a lightweight aluminum rowboat. And to this very day, every time I see a celebrity or senior statesman on television "christening" a ship or a yacht by smashing a bottle of champagne across its bow, I think of Daddy; of how he ceremoniously named our rowboat *Krissy* one Saturday afternoon in our backyard by rummaging around in the garage and printing my childhood nickname in bright red letters on the right side of our boat in his best, forward-leaning italic script, dipping one of my "art in a box" paintbrushes into a pint-size can of waterproof Duron paint from Sears Roebuck.

N ext, my oldest sister, Joann, treads the water memories with me, going *way* back in time. The bonding-friendship-fishing theme continues to resonate, creating a vivid, watercolor portrait of our father.

For Jo, it was ice fishing.

"Ice fishing!" she exclaimed with a happy laugh, remembering.

"This was when I was a little *bitty* girl. I remember that it was very, very cold," she says, the sound of a shiver in her voice.

"The kind of cold where everything is absolutely quiet. All I could hear was the sound of Daddy's little saw cutting a circular hole into the ice. That, and the sound of my boots crunching against the hardened snow around our fishing hole."

Good *Lord,* was my father creative: Dock fishing, boat fishing, ice fishing, all so that he could spend solitary time with each of us and share with us one of his favorite pastimes.

She continued:

"Even though I was only four or five, I remember thinking that Daddy was trying to make me feel like I was a very real and very important part of the entire experience, which is why he gave me my own pole. Not a real pole, I don't think—I probably would have been too small to hold it—but one of his makeshift contraptions, like a stick with some string, or maybe even just a piece of string by itself. Whatever it was, I dropped it down into the water and peered down at our dark little hole in the ice. I just remember being so excited—and cold—even though I knew no fish in his right mind would come up to our little hole and bite our hooks."

Jo warms to the icy memories: "After a while, I remember getting a little impatient, maybe even a little bored. So I started skipping and sliding around on the ice, making all of this noise with my boots on the snow, until Daddy finally said something like, 'Be still, Joann Clark! You're going to scare all the fish away with that noise!'"

Ice fishing. I imagined fur boots and igloos. Cold winds.

But because I now realize what Daddy was doing with us, I feel an incredible sense of warmth as well.

M y sister Noelle is one of the most insightful, intuitive people I know in this world. When I talked to her to see if she, too, had any "water stories" to share about Daddy, her words were clear and concise—almost as if she'd been waiting and expecting me to ask.

"Only a few weeks ago," Noelle said, "I had a very spiritual experience with Daddy. I felt his presence more strongly than I have since he died."

This is a woman who swims a zillion laps a week. She is a fish, or better yet, a beautiful brown mermaid.

"I was swimming when Daddy came to 'visit.' Suddenly, Daddy was swimming right alongside me, matching me stroke for stroke."

"What struck me most as he swam beside me was how healthy and strong he was," she said of Dad's recent powerful, spiritual visit.

Noelle was right. Until the moment he died, at eighty-two years old, Daddy was as strong as an ox; active and nimble (he'd break into a spontaneous dance step, usually a soft-shoe, in our yellow kitchen at *least* two or three times a week), a lifeguard in his youth, and, of course, a fisherman of fishermen.

Noelle continued to describe her recent spiritual visit with Daddy:

"As I was swimming through the water, I began thinking about how healthy Daddy kept all of us when we were children, and about how seriously he took this responsibility."

"Although this was long before you came along, Krissy, Daddy would make us this wonderful oatmeal. He'd throw in a little bit of everything— whatever he could find in the kitchen that would provide us sustenance throughout the day. It was Daddy who first conceived the idea of 'gourmet oatmeal' as we know it today," she said, her voice smiling.

"He'd throw in raisins, bananas, chunks of apple, nuts—whatever we had in the cupboard or refrigerator. To us, it was simply natural. We loved it!"

Excited now, her mind took both of us back: "And do you remember how he tried to make exercise so much of a normal part of our lives that we didn't even realize we were working so hard?"

"Long before you came along, he'd gather us together and we'd all walk over to Grandma's.

"Even though the trip was about four or five miles, we didn't see it as an imposition. We saw it as wonderful time with our father. Little did we know he was training us, even then, to be healthy. To be strong. He was building our stamina. That's why I think he came back to visit me recently; to make sure I was still staying strong.

"And he came to make sure I still loved the water," she added, as if in afterthought.

"How could I *not* still love the water?" she asked, incredulity in her voice. "As many bridges, docks, boats, and piers that Daddy and I have fished from? How could I not?" Sweet sadness filled her voice. (Noelle missed Daddy a lot, as do all of us, but she and Dad had shaped a special relationship. And sadly, it had been Noelle who'd walked into our house one August afternoon to find Daddy dead, slumped over in a chair in the hallway from a heart attack.)

When Daddy retired, Noelle bought him a big, beautiful new boat as a retirement gift. A tribute and a "thank you," she said, to our father for all the wonderful moments we spent together on the water. (I must admit: this boat was a far, far cry from our old aluminum rowboat named *Krissy*. It even had an engine—a big one, too!—not like the two wooden oars we used for our rowboat. This boat was wide in girth, heavy enough to "drop anchor," with shiny red leather seats and a wooden steering wheel that made Daddy smile a smile that was as wide as the Detroit River.)

Said Noelle of her boat gift to Dad:

"It was my way of giving back to Daddy what he so lovingly gave to all of us: tender, fun-filled moments on the water."

It was a gift of love.

With the big new boat, Daddy could fit more of us on board at once. Cruising down the Detroit River, chest puffed out with pride, he'd wave a casual hello to all of his fisherman friends, friends whom he'd known for years. But this time, he was the captain. He was the *man*. Otis Redding, move on over, because for Daddy, there was no more "sitting on the dock of the bay." He was the King of the Detroit River. All his friends waved back from the shore, holding up their catches of the day for Daddy to admire. Daddy looked, but he didn't really see. His vision was too obscured by his happiness, as was ours.

So the gift we were given was this: a father who knew the value of stamina and strength; of catching a pike without letting him go; of making gourmet oatmeal long before Quaker Oaks even knew there could be such a thing; and of the goodness of "power-walking" (eight or nine miles, round-trip, to Grandma's house) *long* before health spas even came into vogue.

Although my sweet sister Ingrid required a *little* longer than my other siblings to rustle her water memories and allow them to bubble up to the surface, eventually, she did. (Ingrid is my best friend. I love her deeply, and I tell her that all the time.) At first, she thought there weren't any water stories that she shared with Dad. But then, finally, a wave of a memory splashed into her consciousness:

"I didn't realize until you and I sat down to talk—until I had a chance to really reflect on it—that Dad's fishing trips with me were *meant* to be customized and fun-filled," she said.

"Now that I think about it, I *do* remember sitting on the banks of the Detroit River with Dad at Belle Isle, waiting for what seemed like hours for us to even get a nibble."

The memories were bubbling up fast now.

"While Daddy was sitting there, still as a statue, waiting for a bite, I'd be climbing trees and running all around the park," she said. "I used to wonder how on earth he could *sit* there for so long, waiting on *one* fish."

I smiled.

"On one particular Saturday," Inny said, "I remember thinking to myself, *Can't we just go home now?* I knew Daddy had a million things to do back home," she said.

The memories came flooding back like it was yesterday.

"For one, he had to patch the busted inner tube on my bike. And Saturdays were always lawn-mowing days. Plus, he and Mother were having a card party that particular night, and whenever Scottie and Gerta came over [my parents' best friends who were also their poker buddies], Daddy would always make the knickknacks to eat. Never mind that he usually had to work the double shift on weekends," she went on.

"What I remember about fishing with Daddy is feeling more perplexed than anything. . . . How could he sit still for so long, knowing all that must have been going on at home without him?

"But now that I reflect, I realize that it was Daddy who gave me my first true glimpse of an African American man who was actually capable of placing himself into a total, undeniable state of deep, sustained relaxation," she said.

"I marvel, now, at the complete state of tranquillity Daddy used to create for himself and for me, and at how magically transformed he would become when he was fishing—almost like he was meditating. He almost became one with nature."

"I'm sure I learned the concept of transcendence and the beauty of tranquillity from Daddy—from fishing!" she said.

This, too, was decades before words like "tranquillity" and "transcendence" were even part of the American lexicon, particularly as they related to black men.

I think of a recent class I took in the serenity of a Zen studio. The class was called "Seijaku," which means *stillness in the midst of chaos.*

Dad, always ahead of his time, could have taught this ultramodern class seven decades ago.

Blindfolded.

I only wish I could have witnessed more clearly the first time Daddy took my own two children fishing, but tears were stinging my eyes and I didn't want to cause an emotional, sappy scene.

I had the presence of mind, thank the Lord, to bring my camera, and I shot rolls and rolls of film while they fished. I needed to capture this multigenerational moment in time, even though Daddy fussed at me about

My father, James Clark, known as "Daddy Jim" to his grandchildren, sharing priceless moments on the banks of Belle Isle in Detroit, teaching my children, Lonnie Paul and Mary Elizabeth, the fine art of fishing

all the noise I was making with my camera and warned me that I'd scare the fish away.

Even as I was obediently putting my camera away (I'd already taken most of the shots I needed anyway), I was already certain of this immutable fact: Daddy's "water stories" had trickled down to an entirely new generation, to my own children and my sisters' and brothers' children. There's no denying it: Daddy is now gone, but his passion—for creating lasting friendships with his children and the joy of reeling in that twelve-pound pike—remains alive in every one of our hearts.

Which is exactly what he intended.

The Six Words That Can Destroy a Father-Child Relationship: "I'm Your **Father**—**Not** Your Friend!"

I wince every time I hear a father say to his child, "You're talking to me like I'm your brother or one of your friends at school. . . . Let's get these roles straight, right here and right now: *I'm your **father**, **not** your friend!* "

My one-word reaction:

"Hogwash."

African American children need all the nurturing, male mentoring, and pure paternal friendship they can get. And from who best, if not their own fathers? As I've mentioned earlier, many black men have not traditionally been required to play the dual role of both provider and nurturer, an absence, I believe, that has done the entire family unit a grave disservice. Yes, this dual-role requirement is certainly a tall order, but it is one that can be fulfilled. Can't we help our black fathers learn to play both roles effectively? Why must we draw such a dramatic, insurmountable divide between the two paternal roles?

Whenever a black father refuses to play the role of "friend" to his child, opting instead to play the sole role of provider and disciplinarian, it spells certain doom for his relationship with his child. It compromises the father-child relationship and erects destructive barriers and roadblocks that will prevent the child from learning to develop strong, healthy friendships with others in his life. This kind of social and emotional deprivation also seals the fate of both the child and the father; it assures that neither will ever know the warmth and wonder of a true father-child friendship.

A father who lets his *machismo* get in the way of his ability to nurture and befriend his own child is a father whose inability to balance the various roles in his life (provider, nurturer, friend, etc.) poisons his relationship with his children.

It requires both a clarity of vision and an uncompromisingly strong sense of self-worth for a father to also be a friend to his child. It requires strength. Fortitude. A proper sense of balance and proportionality. My father had it. Many, many other black fathers have it, particularly in these contemporary times. But at this point in our African American culture, I believe it is an acquired skill rather than an instinctive one.

When W.E.B. Du Bois accurately predicted in *The Souls of Black Folk* that "the negro race, like all races, is going to be saved by its exceptional men," I'm fairly certain he was defining as "exceptional" those men who are not only leaders, but who are also willing to be led; as fathers, perhaps, who are willing to learn to be friends to their children; as men who are strong enough to lead *and* love their own progeny.

Sadly, there are too many black fathers who don't know—or are unwilling to try to learn (in any appreciably demonstrative sense)—how to *show* the love they feel for their children in deliberate, purposeful ways; who rule with an iron hand and a cold, uncompromising heart.

I think of Walt Whitman's stinging description of the father who knows nothing about nurturing his children or holding them in a long and loving embrace. I put forward Whitman's observation here to show fathers and fathers-to-be exactly what they do *not* want to become in their children's eyes:

> *The father . . . manly, mean, anger'd, unjust,*
> *The blow, the quick loud word, the tight bargain, the crafty lure.*

Whitman's passage fills my mind with questions and, I must admit, a prickling of fear beginning at the nape of my neck: Why must a father be "mean" to his child at all? What benefit is derived from his feeling, in Whitman's words, "angered" and "unjust" toward his children?

I think of my own father and how startlingly different he was from Whitman's description of fathers offering their children "tight bargains," "loud words," and "crafty lures." I smile when I think of the "lures" my father offered his children.

It takes my siblings and me to describe the "lures" Daddy used with us. What kind of lures were they?

They were the shiny, rubbery, neon-colored fishing lures kept in his tackle box; the better with which to attract pikes, perch, trout—and, of course, his own children.

The Father with Fangs

In his book *Fatherless America*, David Blankenhorn compares the "Old Father" with the "New Father" by examining their comparative ability (or inability) to nurture and provide friendship to their children.

Blankenhorn describes the "Old Father" as one who was "busy remaining physically and emotionally distant from his family."

He continues with his vivid description: "The 'Old Father' wields power," he says. "He controls. He decides. He tells other people what to do. He 'has fangs'. . . . This aspect of his character generates suspicion and resentment; sometimes from his wife, frequently from his children, and, increasingly, from the larger society as well."

The "New Father," on the other hand, as Blankenhorn draws the picture, represents, with some relief, "fatherhood, finally, with a human face."

"He is a healer, a companion, a colleague," Blankenhorn describes. He, too, clearly believes that these nurturing qualities are beneficial. But balancing the competing roles of "authoritarian and provider" with "friend and nurturer" is key—and the role of authoritarian should *never* be dropped. That, he says, would be a mistake.

I agree.

I believe that there is a happy medium, although elusive and mercurial, which black fathers can and must establish with their children that balances out their role as provider-authoritarian with their role as nurturer-friend. One role need not offset, negate, or even compromise the other. If anything, the two roles should complement each other, for the good of the child and the father as well.

D r. Karen Noelle Clark, a Detroit psychologist who also happens to be my sister, makes this observation about the black father's delicate "balancing act" as both father and friend.

"Daddy's magic came largely from his own willingness and acceptance to play a complementary role in his family's life. That in and of itself—especially so many years ago, when the black father was typically burdened by so many other obstacles as he went about the task of raising and providing for his family—is what made him so unique among black fathers."

She continued, again, both as psychologist and as sister: "It is perfectly clear to me, *long* before any of us came along, that Mother and Daddy made the conscious decision to dedicate their entire lives to their children," she said. "Before we were even thought of they'd already decided.

"Daddy decided that, in order to give Mother the support she needed to pursue her own dreams and in order to create lasting, distinctive relationships with each of his children, that he was going to adopt this additional, *complementary* role."

She was quick to make the following vital distinction, as should we all:

"Not a *secondary* role, mind you," she added deliberately, "but a *complementary* role."

In essence, what I am now saying to black fathers and black families everywhere is precisely what Noelle was saying to me. We are two women who have been blessed to have had a mother and father who loved us in large, gulping doses.

"We knew," Noelle said, "with every fiber of our being, that both of our parents loved us unconditionally, and that they put us first in everything they did. There was never any question. It was just a *given*. An absolute. Even if it meant Dad had to shift roles a bit here and there along the way: if it meant that shifting his roles somehow created a better world for *us*, then he was going to do it. No matter what."

She continued, "This complementary role is a very difficult one for a black father to play, because implicit in the word 'complementary' is the assumption that it also means 'subservient' or 'weak.' For many, playing a complementary role seems, somehow, beneath them. They're threatened that it may undermine their authority or masculinity."

"I see it in my clients all the time. The entire issue has much more to do with how one sees himself as a *man*—how deep his own self-esteem runs, than how he sees himself as a father."

◆

Poet Robert Frost, in a light moment, reflects:

"You don't have to deserve your mother's love.
You have to deserve your father's. He's more particular."

◆

In other words, a mother's love and her accompanying friendship is a *given*, as natural and instinctive as breathing.

Why must a father's love for his children be any less instinctive and demonstrable?

The "Forever Friend": Does Such a Thing Still Exist?

Scottie Longmeyer was my father's best friend.

They were poker buddies; fishing companions; solid friends who loved their wives, their children, and each other with slow-burning intensity. They'd spend hours at the local hardware store comparing gizmos and garden hoses, widgets and wood putty, fishing line and flashlights. They drove each other to their doctors' appointments (and, yes, occasionally to the racetrack).

The importance of black male-on-male friendships (friendships that exist outside of and distinct from the family unit, I should point out) is that they are empowering and symbiotic: certainly, every black father needs that *one lifelong* best friend whom he can "open up" with, play cards with, or talk to. I remember well, in my youth, watching my father and his best friend sitting on our front porch together, listening to a Detroit Tigers game on the radio. Male-male friendships are a good thing in that each party gets something out of it: the comforting knowledge that a valued and trusted relationship can indeed exist outside of the confines of the family unit, and the warmth and unconditional comfort that come with simply having a best friend.

Nurturing a lasting male-male friendship outside of the home enables a black father to more adeptly strengthen his familial relationships inside of the home. But women and wives, take heed: if you are comfortable and secure enough in your relationship with your husband or partner, then you must encourage and enable your man to keep his "best friendship" alive, no matter how much it may hurt your semifragile ego or how lonely it makes you feel when you see him stepping happily out the door to shoot hoops—or even just the breeze—with his best friend; and in many cases, the friend he has known long before he even knew *you*. Female partners play a pivotal role in enabling their men to maintain their male "best friendships."

Mother loved Scottie as much as my father did; and she loved Scottie not only because he was Scottie.

But because he was my father's best friend.

For this chapter on friendship, I wanted desperately to speak with Scottie; to ask my father's best male friend what made their relationship so special; to probe and peek into his mind, if only for a moment; to uncover the secret of how two men (both tremendously dedicated, loving black fathers) could maintain such a close friendship for more than seventy years.

On a recent cloudy afternoon, Scottie's wife, Gerta, explained to me that, although he'd just celebrated his one-hundredth birthday, Scottie could no longer really speak and had lost virtually all of his hearing. Gerta explained that Scottie had recently tossed his hearing aid in the trash can (the exact same thing my father would have done had he reached the point of needing one) because, in her words, "The silly thing didn't work well and Scottie always had to end up screaming, which he absolutely hates."

I could imagine Scottie tossing his plastic hearing aid gracefully into the white trash bin in their kitchen, his auditory senses compromised, but his dignity still very much intact.

But Gerta turned out to be my saving grace: to help me write this section of the book, Gerta tried every which way but upside down to devise a plan that would somehow allow Scottie to share his feelings and memories about Daddy with me—that is, if any of those memories still remained. Gerta herself remains full of life and is quick to laugh. It lit up my heart to be able to talk to her again after so many years.

"I remember when Mary died," Gerta said, referring to my mom. "When she died, a part of me died right along with her."

I inhaled deeply, bracing myself for the darkness. I didn't want to relive those paralyzing moments just after Mother's death, but Gerta wanted to talk about it, so I listened, out of respect and love; both for Mother and for Gerta.

"Your mom's death was hard on Scottie, too, but for different reasons," she said.

"Of course, Scottie loved your mother like a sister, but he was more concerned about how your *dad* was taking Mary's death. He was so very worried about how—and if—your dad would survive without her."

Scottie Longmeyer, the faithful friend: it had never really occurred to me that after Mother's death, I, for one, was so wrapped up in my own paralyzing pain that I forgot to remember Daddy and all that he must have been going through. I forgot. . . . But not Scottie.

"Scottie was most worried about your father after all the hubbub of the funeral had died down and all the out-of-town visitors had flown home and all the condolence cards had been gathered up and tucked away."

"I could see the worry and the pain in his face, and he'd just pace the floor of our bedroom at night, back and forth, back and forth. I'll never forget it," she said sadly. "Scottie was most worried when your father finally had to face a house—and a life—without your mother."

Gerta's voice caught just a tiny bit, but she continued: "Scottie would call or drop by your daddy's house just about every day—this was after you'd gone back to Washington and everybody had pretty much gotten back into the swing of their own lives again," she explained.

I said a prayer of thanks to Scottie, a prayer that was long, long overdue.

"He'd call your house just about every day and say, 'J.J., you feelin' okay? [J.J. was Scottie's nickname for Daddy.] You want to go down to the hardware store tomorrow? I need a new water valve for the downstairs bathroom, and you know you're the only one who can help me with that stubborn ol' toilet.' "

Why *wouldn't* a man try to comfort his best friend and keep him busy when the loneliness of losing his soul mate became too much to bear? Gerta's observation helped me appreciate, in a much deeper sense, the value of male-male relationships.

She continued, her voice sounding slightly befuddled, but not at all bitter:

"The odd thing was that Scottie never really asked me how *I* was doing with Mary's death. He wasn't trying to be mean to me or ignore me, it's just that he knew how much your father loved your mom—and he certainly knew in his own heart how much he loved your father—and that was all he could really think about," she said.

Gerta graciously agreed to try to figure out some way to ask Scottie about Daddy within the next few weeks, even if it meant her having to frame the questions so that Scottie could just nod "yes" or "no."

"I'll need some time on this one," she said before hanging up.

But she agreed to try. It might have been as important to her as it was to me, the task of trying to reach into the darkened recesses of her husband's mind.

A few weeks later, I called her back. For some reason, I felt breathless and jittery as I dialed her number. As soon as she picked up the phone I realized the source of my jangled nerves: I didn't even want to face the prospect of what Gerta was going to say. I didn't want to entertain the possibility that Scottie might not remember anything about my father, that the moments and memories and decades of their friendship had finally faded to black.

But it was Gerta herself who cut right through our "how's-the-weather" small talk and got right to the point.

"Something strange happened last night," she said.

A few drops of perspiration sprang onto my nose. All I could do was hold the phone and listen.

"I've been talking to Scottie about J.J. these past two weeks. You know, just kind of talking out loud about J.J., more to myself than anyone, hoping Scottie could hear me or was listening. I even pulled out a few old photos of the four of us together at your house, playing cards or sitting in the kitchen. When Scottie looked at the photos, something told me he remembered," she said.

A tiny flicker of hope danced around in my heart.

"I thought you might be interested in this," Gerta said.

"Yesterday, I watched Scottie just sitting in his wheelchair, holding a flashlight in his lap, of all things."

"A flashlight?" was all I could muster as a follow-up question. I swear I was too overcome to get anything else out of my mouth.

But Gerta went on. "Yes, a flashlight," she said, obviously surprised herself by Scottie's behavior.

"There he was, sitting in our bedroom in broad daylight, holding this big flashlight in his lap. I recognized the flashlight because it was the same one he's been keeping in the top drawer of his dresser for as long as I can remember. All these years, I never really paid that old flashlight any mind. Not until yesterday, when I saw Scottie had actually reached into the drawer and picked it up."

She continued, "I said to Scottie, 'What in the world are you doing with that flashlight, Mr. Longmeyer?' "

Gerta described the flashlight as one of those big metal camping flashlights, almost too heavy for Scottie to lift by himself.

I couldn't help wondering myself. *A flashlight?*

Finally she mustered up an answer from Scottie.

The woman had a heart of gold and the determination of Job.

"New batteries," he said.

"Can you *imagine*? Now that he'd mentioned it, I *do* remember J.J. giving Scottie that flashlight for a birthday gift; but that was years ago. I think J.J. got it at the hardware store where the two of them used to shop, and that was thirty or forty years ago.

"Here's something else," she said into the phone like a detective on the prowl.

"Last night, I was talking about J.J. again to Scottie at the dinner table, and he just wheeled away from the table, heading toward the bedroom.

"So I followed him into the bedroom," she said with a sound of genuine concern in her voice, "because I thought he looked unusually tired. I knew he was too tired to speak and didn't feel like having me yelling in his face, so I grabbed a pad of paper and wrote down the words 'What's wrong?' "

Scottie shook his head, indicating nothing was wrong.

"But I could tell something was setting on his mind," she said. "So I figure I'd push it one last time, then leave it alone."

She was as tenacious as a bulldog, Gerta was.

"I had a feeling he'd been thinking about your dad, so I wrote down the words, 'What do you remember about J.J.?' "

Perspiration beads popped back onto my nose. Hot air swam around my head.

Gerta continued, "He still didn't say anything, so I rewrote the question so he wouldn't have to answer in a full sentence. This time, I wrote a simple, yes-or-no question:

"Do you remember J.J.?"

The hair at the nape of my neck stood at full, prickly attention as I listened for the response. I was actually *holding my breath*.

"What'd he write down, Gerta?" I asked. It was just about all I could get out.

"He wrote down two words," she said. "Two words that I thought you'd certainly want to hear."

It felt like I was eating cotton, or as if someone had stuffed my ears with a cupful of cumulus clouds.

"You know what he wrote?" Gerta asked rhetorically. Her pause seemed to last a lifetime.

"He wrote down the words 'best friend.'

"So yes, baby," she said tenderly. "Now you know that Scottie *does* remember J.J., and that he still considers J.J. his best friend. Put that in your book and let it teach others about the value of true friendship."

Not old age, nor the passage of time, nor even death can break the bond of true friendship.

"Best friends."

I'll let these two words speak for themselves.

What follows is another personal testimony from a young person about his father's strong paternal influence and friendship. The words of Austin Dabney, ten years old when he shared this story, are aglow with pride and passion. The words are his own, pure and simple in their power. His father, Kevin Dabney, is a rescue specialist stationed in Falls Church, Virginia, and was one of the first rescue workers called to the scene at the Pentagon on the morning of September 11, 2001, only moments after the hijacked aircraft plunged into the building, instantly killing hundreds.

A Hero Lies in You!

The first thing I want to say about my father is that he is my friend and he is my hero. He's not only a real-life hero to me, and to my little brother, Ian, and to my mom, whose name is Melissa, but he is a hero to lots of other people who don't even know his name because he worked so hard at the Pentagon on September 11.

There have been so many times my mom, my brother, and I

have met Dad at the airport as he's come home from doing rescue work from far-off places around the world! He's been called to Taiwan and to Iceland and to Turkey, too. Remember when they had that huge earthquake in Turkey? Well, I saw my dad on television pulling a little boy out of that earthquake— and a lady, too. I saw it on the news, and when Dad came home safely from that trip to Turkey, I felt really, really lucky. You know why? Because my dad told me that the little boy he pulled out was eight years old—about the same age as I was at that time.

A hero's welcome: Austin and his little brother, Ian, greet their father, Kevin Dabney, a firefighter who was among the first to arrive at the Pentagon on September 11, 2001

Whenever Dad comes home from a trip like that, my mom always helps Ian and I make a big poster right before we go to meet him, and she's always taking lots of pictures of us. Usually, she's crying, because she's so proud and she's so happy that Dad got home safely.

Dad spent a full week at the Pentagon after the attacks. He couldn't even come home, but he called whenever he could. He was doing whatever he needed to do to save people's lives. In the picture my mom took [above], that's me holding up the poster that says *Welcome Home, Dad*, with two American flags, and my brother Ian is standing beside me holding the poster that says, *My Daddy's a Hero*. When he came home, I really felt very proud. And also very happy because as soon as I saw his face, I knew he was safe.

At my dad's "office"

In our house, our family says "I love you" a whole lot. My parents say it to us all the time, and Ian and I say it to our mom and dad, too. When my dad calls from wherever he is—and sometimes he'll call home from this cool, special hotline they have set up for the rescue workers who want to talk to their families for just a minute—he always ends the conversation with "I love you." I know he does, too. He says it and he means it: even when he's not doing something very dangerous, he still loves me very much.

My dad got the call to come right to the Pentagon on September 11, right after the explosion, and he worked without stopping or even coming home straight through until September 18. It's funny, because my birthday is on September 27, and he didn't miss my birthday—and his birthday is on September 20, which meant he was home for both of our birthdays even though so much was going on in the world. In fact, a few days after he got home safely from the Pentagon, my family and I got on a plane and flew to Orlando and to Universal Studios. We had been planning for this trip for a long time, and we didn't want to let anyone or anything—not even terrorists—have enough power to make us change our plans. So we got on that plane anyway—even though it was completely empty. I knew I was safe because I was with my dad and my mom, so I didn't worry. We had a great time—and there weren't even any crowds at any of the parks. Dad was pretty tired while we were there, but he kind of made himself have a good time because he knew it was important to the family. The most important thing to me was that my entire family was together again. Safe and sound.

My dad is definitely my best friend. He's usually gone for a whole week out of the month, doing his rescue work. But the funny thing is that even when he's gone, it still feels like he's right there. Right around the house. He'll call from wherever he is and say something like, "How's everything going at home?" or "Are my two boys taking good care of their mother?" or something like that.

When he's home, we also love watching and playing sports. He teaches me how to "play smart" when I play certain sports. Like for instance, he'll teach me how to figure out where the ball is headed before it gets to where it's going. He teaches me how to be safe when I'm playing and how not to get myself injured. He's very, very smart about safety and things like that. Yesterday, we were working on lacrosse. Even though he's not really all that great at playing lacrosse, he still knows how to teach me to be safe when I play. Same with baseball and basketball. My dad is really good at teaching me how to "think safe." He teaches me that it's not all about scoring the most points, but how to play the game right and how not to get hurt.

He also comes to visit our school sometimes [for Career Day]. I really like this photo [right] of my dad coming to visit Ian's preschool class. It's one of my mom's favorite pictures, too.

After he taught all the kids [in class] about fire safety and "stop, drop and roll," he all of a sudden had this urge to give Ian a big hug. So he hugged him right there in the classroom, even with his gas mask and his

Father Kevin, in partial uniform, reaches down to hug his son Ian—oxygen tank, gas mask and all—after participating in Career Day at his son's school

I want to be just like my dad when I grow up!

oxygen tank strapped to his back! We're pretty used to him giving us big hugs even when he's wearing all of his equipment. We're just so proud of him—and so glad he's staying safe—that hugging him is mostly what we like to do best.

My mom, my brother, and I visit him at his rescue station whenever we can. He'll let Ian and I climb up on the fire truck and even wear his special equipment if there's enough time. That equipment looks really light on him, but on me, it feels like it weighs a ton! Even when I was little, I remember my mom taking me to the station to see him and to see all the things he does.

As long as I can remember, my dad and my mom have always been there for us. Always. So, I really, truly know that my father is my best friend. My mom definitely is, too, because she's the one who helps us try not to worry when Dad's gone—even though I know she's worried, too, but she tries not to show it.

He's the biggest hero I know. And you know what? I thought he was a hero a long time before September 11!

as told by Austin Dabney, 10

Fathers: cherish the friendship between you and your child, and work hard to keep it alive. This facilitates a healthy heart and a smiling soul. It allows you to bring your own children closer in around you, teaching them the inherent value of friendship. Teach your children, through your own actions, about the joy of lasting friendships. Commit yourself to being their best friend. Hold their hands tightly. Hug them when you get a hankering. Tickle their toes. There is beauty to be found in the tickling of a child's toes.

"TICKLE, TICKLE"

Are you ticklish?

me papa tickle me feet
he call it "finger treat"
me scream and run each time he come
me papa tickle me feet

he tickle me tummy, me chest, me arm
his fingers fly so wild
he say, "Come here, little man.
You my ticklin' chile."

me papa say he love me
me papa look so proud
he say, "Sonny, what a joy
to see you laugh out loud."

he tickle me ribs, me neck, me back
his fingers grow longer each day
me twist and swing and laugh and kick
but he hold me anyway

me eyes, they water
me throat be sore
me weak, me dizzy
but me want more

he throw me high up in the air
and catch me from behind

me say, "Go higher!" and he say,
"Don't you know you're mine?"

me papa tickle me feet
he call it "finger treat"
me scream and run (but, OH WHAT FUN!)
when papa tickle me feet
—DAKARI HRU,
FROM *IN DADDY'S ARMS I AM TALL*

5.

JOINING HANDS TO
RE-CREATE COMMUNITIES

THE IMPORTANCE OF A HOLISTIC,
COMMUNAL APPROACH
TO FAMILIES AND FATHERHOOD

Our developing African American communities will be what shapes the direction of our families and, indeed, our futures. Ironically, integration and the civil rights struggles of the sixties—as useful as they were at the time—simultaneously struck a harmful blow to the solidity and structural integrity of the black family. Highways cut through communities. Busing brought along with it anxiety and separation. Moving out to "the suburbs"—getting away from our own people to live "in comfort" with white people—was how we began to measure our success. Visiting your best friend became a twenty-minute car ride instead of a thirty-second dash across the street. The "we-ness" disappeared, and, along with it, the fabric of our families began to unravel at the seams.

Family dynamics began to change. Divorce rates rose. Single-parent households became more the norm than the exception. Because we were now more isolated from each other, our collective, communal values were dangerously diminished. The only thing that kept us going, unfortunately, that kept us moving and motivated, was trying to get a bigger piece of the pie, even if it meant destroying ourselves in the process.

Kind of like the proverbial crabs in a barrel.

This chapter looks at our lost communities, and at the black father's place in that community. It will offer substantive solutions we can begin considering as options, to bring back all that we have lost.

The yesterdays of our lives might have been painful at times, but our cohesion and collective caring seemed to slice, somewhat, through the pain, straight to our hearts, where the warmth was.

———◆———

So, also, says former U.S. Congressperson Barbara Jordan:

"We were all black and we were all poor and were all right there in place. For us, the larger community didn't exist."

———◆———

Paul Robeson also celebrated that same
connectedness within the black community:

"What I remember most was an abiding
sense of comfort and security.
I got plenty of mothering, not only from Pop
and my brothers and sisters when they were home,
but from the whole of our close-knit community."

———◆———

Jordan and Robeson were celebrating the very thing that we should be trying to re-create: strong, self-sufficient black communities that uplift and protect us; communities that place the black father back at the head of the table and place the family unit under the same roof.

So put on your walking shoes, because our trek toward togetherness is going to be a long one.

When we were small, my backyard and my best friend Cookie's backyard shared a chain-link fence. "Shared" is the word I use deliberately, because rather than *dividing* us, this fence provided countless hours of shared joy; shared experiences; shared moments of untold, spontaneous, youthful, and often reckless abandon. This wire wall provided us the chance to be creative. It gave us the chance to figure out innovative (and sometimes painful) ways to traverse it. When I was young, there was precious little that divided me from my neighborhood, from my community. More important, and on a much more universal scale, there was precious little that divided us *from each other*. Without a doubt, the forces were with us. They bound us together, kept us close; showered us with that comforting, collective sense of belonging and certainty, as if we existed within the center of a high-powered magnetic field.

We were our own center of gravity.

During my childhood, there were no "fences" to speak of within my neighborhood. Only friendships. An occasional feud. Looking back at the twilight of my youth, I recognize now that I was not forced to face any threats—real or perceived—to life and limb, as is pervasive in today's fractured black communities. During my youth, the only real challenge we ever faced was that old backyard fence; figuring out how best to twist and turn our sneakered feet "just right" in order to fit them into the wire holes, simultaneously wrapping our fingers around the double-twisted wire and slowly hoisting ourselves up—left hand, right foot; right hand, left foot—until we reached the top. We weren't worried about protecting life and limb back then; we didn't *need* to be. It just wasn't a part of our reality. We did not know that kind of fright.

What we *did* know, with certainty and pride, was that we were adventurers. We were *conquerors*, even if the only thing we conquered was our backyard fence. We weren't malicious: we were *mountain climbers,* for goodness' sake. Our backyard chain-link fence represented the Mount Everest of our youth and our dreams, even if it only meant figuring out how to conquer the gravitational challenges of our own fence.

Our fences *kept us in,* close around each other.

Today they are built to keep us apart, separated and isolated from each other.

Our magnetic field has disappeared.

I ask this question to readers about my age or older (we'll say forty-something and above); a question that will require you to still yourself, reach back, and remember: can you recall the communal safety net that used to catch you, unfailingly, every time you looked like you were about to veer off in the wrong direction? Or, when you did something terribly, life-threateningly wrong, you could *bank on* getting not only a switch across the back of your legs from your *own* parents, but from Mrs. Russell (maybe Mr. Russell, too) who lived down the block and actually saw you do it? Remember when you—when all of us—could romp and run with youthful abandon? When the only fear we really ever experienced had nothing to do with a sudden burst of gunfire or the prospect of a random, rage-filled drive-by shooting? When the only fear you ever really knew was when Mr. McFall or Mr. White or whoever your own childhood Mr. "Fill-in-the-Blank" was in your own community would yell at you through his screen window to stay off of his grass—and even then, over all his loud yelling and crotchety ways, you knew he really loved you as much as he loved his own children? When every boy on your block had a "family" of fathers and every girl had as many mothers as there were women on the street?

Those days are much more than warm memories for me. They are a vital part of the person I have become. I carry the sights, the smells, the sound of laughter, the smell of the lilac and lavender—*all* of it—around with me, deep inside that place that has become the person who I am, a living testament to the world in which I lived and the values that we cherished.

No, we cannot travel back in time to those days, but we can and *must* try to re-create the resin that bound our fathers, nuclear families, and extended families together in the spirit of community and love. Those days of our youth must become more than mere sentimental memories. They should be road maps and recipes that we share with our children constantly, to teach them—through our own experiences—the precise ingredients they'll need to make those heaping, holistic dishes of communal love and laughter. For this reason, it becomes vital that we share our own childhood experiences and values with our children. You'll read these words in my book again as they pertain to the solidity of the black family unit: for us to move forward, we *must* look back.

Look back at the yesterdays of our childhood, when doing the right thing was what was expected and doing wrong was simply intolerable. When the black community was bound together closely not only because we had to be, but because we *wanted* to be. We took care of each other. Because we were all we had.

When I was small, I remember thinking—no, *believing*—that Cookie's father, James Pounds, had almost as much authority over my well-being and whereabouts as my own father. And she felt the same way about my dad. It wasn't even something we talked about. We just *felt* it, nestled deeply in our hearts and our psyches. We were safe.

Our community of fathers would see to that.

"Black men must make a special effort to become
spiritual and psychological fathers to needy black children
within their extended families and community."
— ALVIN POUSSAINT, PSYCHIATRIST

Dr. Poussaint and I agree on that point, and I will take it a step further: it is the responsibility of every black male to become a father figure of some sort to the children in his community, just as Cookie's father was to me, and my father was to Cookie.

Although many people will find it difficult if not impossible to conceptualize the revitalization of the black community and the strengthening of the black family unit as we once knew it, I still breathe the breath of hope.

Call me naive or claim that my vision is blurred or hopelessly saturated with syrupy sweet sentimentalism. But I hope you don't. Because in order to achieve the collective goal of rebuilding our communities, it requires complete "buy-in" from every member of the community. Ask any architect or design engineer: rebuilding a structure—whether it's a house, a skyscraper, or a community—is infinitely easier if a strong, solid foundation has already been laid; if we are already familiar with its dimensions, its depth, its ability to stand, unyielding, against the strongest winds of adversity and change. Of this much we are sure: as a race of people, we *once* had that strong foundation. The question then becomes, Do we have the tools, the driving desire, the vision, and the resources to rebuild that foundation?

Our decision to rebuild is not really optional. It is mandatory. Our survival depends on it. We alone are the only ones who can manage the task. Why? Because we alone have the shared collective memories; the energy, the capital, and the vision for a new and brighter day.

There are already two, three, maybe even four generations today who have no earthly idea of what a "shared community" really is. They regard the concepts "right" and "wrong" in relative terms rather than the absolute, unchanging values that they are. But we cannot blame them for their ignorance. We can only blame ourselves for not passing along to them the moral absolutes (which *we* ourselves once abided by) and for allowing successive generations to be brought into this world with no sense of moral clarity. When babies have babies and when black teens are killed (most often at the hands of *each other*) before they can reach adulthood, the values, the moral vision, and the absolutes dissolve and, like dinosaurs, eventually become extinct.

Our families and communities are dwindling away at an alarming rate. Dwindling, almost, into extinction.

To survive, we *must* revive the notion of shared community and common concern: When you hurt, we all hurt. When I am in need, we all are in need. When a young girl is gunned down while playing hopscotch at the playground just for being in the wrong place at the wrong time, the entire community grieves.

———◆———

Here is someone who says it better:

"Two months ago I had a nice apartment in Chicago. I had a good job, I had a son. When something happened to the Negroes in the South I said, 'That's their business, not mine.' Now I know how wrong I was. The murder of my son has shown me that what happens to any of us, anywhere in the world, had better be the business of us all."

—MAMIE TILL,
MOTHER OF LYNCHING VICTIM EMMETT TILL

———◆———

It Takes a Village

I know a miracle of a man named Joseph Lekuton. He is a native of Kenya, a distinguished and revered Masai warrior who journeyed years ago to the United States not only out of a deep and abiding love for his community, but to ensure the survival of the tiny, struggling village in which he was raised.

It was the elders of his village who encouraged him to leave. But not forever. Only long enough to get a solid education; long enough to secure a stronger sense of how the larger universe around them survives and thrives; long enough to absorb all of this new information and come back to share this knowledge with his tribe. With his people. With his community.

As it turned out, he came to the United States, received his degrees, and decided to stay "a little longer" to continue cultivating the depth and breadth of his education. Because God is a good God, He instructed Joseph to remain in the States and begin teaching at a private elementary school.

Fortunately, Joseph listened when God spoke.

So when I meet a distinguished Masai warrior who proudly hails from the tiny village of Kamboe in Kenya, and this wonderful man ends up being the much-loved social studies teacher at my son's former elementary school, the Langley School in McLean, Virginia, I know that this is more than luck.

Again, I have been given a gift.

Mr. Lekuton and I have spent many hours discussing the importance of "shared community." He, too, feels strongly about the need to recapture our communities. In fact, that is precisely what he is doing right now, for his own community. For the larger good of his own people. He, too, sees the "bigger picture," this vision that lifts him above the circumstances of his own daily life and allows him to focus entirely on the good of his own community.

In his culture and throughout his childhood, the collective community is deemed more important than any one individual. Males in particular are revered, cherished, and respected—by the entire community—because they are the providers and protectors of the tribe. (Doesn't this have a familiar ring? Didn't the black male—particularly black fathers—at one time hold the revered and respected role as "head of the family"? As the stalwart provider and fierce protector?)

I find myself comparing and contrasting the two cultures. Joseph is devoting his life to keeping his culture—the same culture in which he grew up—intact. As African Americans, we haven't even begun the task of threading the needle that will sew the fabric of our families back together again into one whole cloth.

Perhaps we can borrow both the thread *and* the needle from people like Mr. Lekuton.

Says Joseph: "My mother gave birth to me after the 'short rain.' . . . "No one really knows the exact date when I came into this world."

Here is a man, I think to myself, *who doesn't know the exact day he was born, but who knows beyond the shadow of a doubt precisely what he needs to do to keep his community intact.*

"We were a nomadic tribe, moving constantly from one place to another—wherever there was water for our cattle," Joseph explains. "A few weeks before I was born, the men of the tribe had decided to move our entire community. They had found a new source of water for our cattle—and the cattle, of course, dictated where and when we would move as a community," he says.

"So two days after I was born, I rode on a donkey, strapped to my mother's back, to this new place that would become our village and our new home. That was when my life as a nomad began," he concludes.

At first blush, one might assume that a nomadic tribe would have very little, if any, sense of community; very little sense of collective belonging—given how often they uproot themselves to relocate, and given that the men and fathers are away much of the time, herding cattle.

That is exactly wrong.

In fact, the opposite is true: a nomadic tribe is *extremely* community-driven. It has to be, in order to survive. It is a symbiotic community, where everything and everyone depends upon each other's larger sense of strength and belonging to survive, with a foolproof, formulaic structure constructed something like this: The villagers depended heavily on their cattle; it was the cattle that dictated when and where they moved, based on available water and food supply. The tribe depended on the males to be the protectors and providers; both to the cattle and to their families. (In a very real way, the cattle was more important to keep alive than any one person within the community, and that responsibility fell directly to the men. The leaders. The fathers. The protectors. The warriors.) The women of the village cooked, cleaned, tended to the existing crops, prepared for the return of their men, and created beautiful beadwork and crafts to sell in the neighboring villages and to the occasional tourist. Although they were nomadic, everything in their lives was tightly interwoven, and their sense of community and shared responsibility was—and is—absolute and unwavering.

"This is how it worked in my community," Joseph explains. "We, the males, would be gone for weeks at a time. We were out herding our cattle, finding new parcels of land, and constantly searching for new sources of water. It was expected of us, and it created an amazingly strong bond between the men.

"It's kind of ironic," he muses. "We really didn't spend that much physical time with the rest of the community, even though we were a vital and indispensable part of it, and they depended completely on us for their survival. We were *always* out in the bush."

It was the collective community, particularly the elders, who identified Joseph as "the special one," the one they selected to leave the village and seek external knowledge. That he ended up in the United States at all he considers, in his own words, an "enlightened miracle."

"My entire village could feel the world changing around them, especially the elders," he reflects.

"We were losing our land and our cattle to industrial farming, the villagers [themselves] to the drought, and our children to abject poverty."

I think of my own community as he speaks; of how we once (mistakenly, I now believe) defined the building of new highways and our moving "out to the suburbs" as a measure of our success, when all it really meant, in the end, was further fracturing of the community and an increasingly segmented black society.

"The elders summoned me one day," Joseph says, sharing his own childhood story with pride and a bright smile.

"I still don't know why they chose me," he shrugs with laughing eyes.

He asks me to keep in mind that his village elders were the wisest men he knew—"and they still are"—yet they'd never stepped foot beyond the confines of their own community. But they did know this, according to Joseph, because they saw it with their own eyes: white people, when they visited the village, were the ones who always seemed to have a *solution*; to devise a more strategic way to execute a plan or a better way to build a mousetrap; whether that "mousetrap" was fixing the transmission of one of their own cars, or healing the villagers with the "magic" medicines they brought with them, or even deciphering and analyzing numerical data and geographic and meteorological trends. These white people with the "solutions" came as missionaries. Some came as journalists and writers. But they all came with not necessarily a *better* sense of knowledge but a different, somehow *larger* body of knowledge.

"Go to the United States, where these white men come from," the elders told him. "Absorb and attain all of the things that they know, then bring it back so that we can save ourselves."

That is exactly what Joseph did.

But getting here would not be easy. Money would need to be raised. Resources, already frighteningly meager, would need to be marshaled. So the elders took necessary action: it was the elders who instructed the entire village to stop everything they were doing—even if it meant leaving the cattle uncared-for momentarily—so that the entire community could focus exclusively on how best to assure Joseph safe, secure passage to America. In fact, the communal, altruistic decision was made to sell off some of the village's precious cattle to pay for Joseph's airfare and some new clothing.

What an important lesson we could utilize in our own black communities, I think as he speaks. The lesson of not only doing what is right, but doing what is needed, even if it means sacrifice, for the larger good of the community, and for the very survival of the community itself.

My two children are blessed to have attended a school that actually felt like a family, because, in a very real sense, *it was*. Both of them have attended the Langley School for most of their lives. Our lives were closely tied to Langley, because our children were. Lonnie Paul has since graduated and has become part of a new school family—St. Albans School, in Washington, D.C.—and we have encircled him closely in this new school community as well, making it our own; actively becoming part of an exciting, new, *shared* community of warm and welcoming teachers, parents, faculty, and students. Because we are active parents who want the best for our children (as any parent does), you'll find us on the sidelines at every soccer game; no matter what other competing demands crowd our schedules, we are vocal and visible at all of the parent and family events at school. We are productive, contributing members of a new community that is helping to mold our son's character and future. Because it is a caring community, St. Albans has opened its embrace to include Lonnie Paul—and as Lonnie Paul steps into this close-knit community, the rest of his family follows close behind.

Creating and perpetuating this sense of shared community is vital to a child's developmental, emotional well-being and sense of social connectedness. As parents, we *must* create and perpetuate many different forms of shared communities for our children, exposing them also to communities that are, perhaps, even stronger than their own. Some examples:

- School communities (You must be active in your child's education! Volunteer! Get involved!)
- Church communities (You should participate in family events at your church, or take church trips with your entire family to visit other places and other communities!)
- Neighborhood communities (Go with your entire family into an impoverished neighborhood and, together with your family and a few others, build a playground or spruce up its community center!)

Make your children's sense of community a reality, not a fuzzy abstraction.

When communities face crisis, they are better able to suffer—or even prevent—some of the harshest blows by virtue of the fact that they are facing the crisis together.

They are not alone.

Several years ago, Kenya saw the worst drought in its history. People were dying by the thousands. Cattle were being wiped out across the land. Bacteria flowed freely, like poison, through what little water remained.

"People were lying dead and dying on the sides of the *road*, Kristin," Joseph described in a voice filled with pain and urgency.

"The bodies of men, women, and children lay dead and dying before my very eyes," he said, his voice choking.

"And as if losing our land and our people wasn't enough, we were losing all of our cattle, too. Carcasses were everywhere, covering my beautiful countryside. It was living hell. I knew I had to help."

And help he did.

Through generous donations and subtle, personalized fund-raising efforts he was able to amass not only the financial capital (staggering amounts of contributions came pouring toward him), but the technical resources to fight back. Now, supported and much loved by a community (us!) who lived on the other side of the world, Joseph could do more than merely wring his hands. He was able to galvanize the best engineering and architectural expertise in the world and build an entirely new irrigation system that saved the lives of too many people to count.

By pulling communities and resources together, Joseph was also able to build a new school in Kenya, a boarding school, the likes of which had never been seen in that area.

His face lights up whenever he talks about the new school.

"It has a dormitory, a dining hall, a kitchen, and, of course, classrooms," he explains, using wide, hand-sweeping motions. "Glass windows, electricity, desks, and even ample school supplies. Before this, the children had next to nothing. The books they were using were worn, outdated. Virtually unreadable. How could they become educated when, through no fault of their own, they didn't have the resources to attain that education?"

To see the beautiful country of Kenya, and to provide for our own children a sense of shared community and ancestral connectedness, all four members of my family recently traveled together to Kenya, with Joseph.

Joseph took us home.

Along with several other Langley families, we made the pilgrimage.

Political and religious leaders from the highest levels reached out to embrace us, because we were with Joseph. Educators, students, and official dignitaries stood awaiting our arrival, arms outstretched to greet us, because we were with Joseph.

Wherever we went, masses of people—statesmen, villagers, excited schoolchildren—came out to greet us, because we were with Joseph. Loading ourselves into jeeps and vans, we traveled deep, deep into the bush every day, where the giraffes strolled in their graceful walk, nibbling leaves from the tops of nearby acacia trees. My daughter, Mary Elizabeth, using our family video camera, filmed a lion stalking and killing a wildebeest about fifty yards in front of us. And as if out of nowhere—just about twenty yards in front of us—a family of elephants crossed our path after having romped in a nearby river that flowed beside us. We sat for about ten or fifteen minutes under a "sausage tree," watching in silence and awe as a leopard lay on the lowest limb (about fifteen feet above our heads), licking her paws and lazing in the noonday sun. At Lake Nakuru, on the border of Tanzania, we were again silenced by the beauty of two and a half million flamingos, an incredible, heart-stopping "wall of pink," as Lonnie Paul described it.

In the evening, after our game rides, we'd talk quietly in our tents or simply sit together under the stars, silenced and pleasantly paralyzed by the magnitude of what we'd seen that day. I'll never forget Mary Elizabeth scooting closer to me after a mother-daughter camel ride along the Indian Ocean on the island of Mombasa. She leaned her head gently on my shoulder. I could tell something was stirring in her soul.

It was.

"Doesn't this all feel a little like a dream, Mom?" she asked, emotion and appreciation filling her voice. I put my arm around her, watching the waves of the ocean, uttering a prayer of thanks to my Lord and Savior for allowing us this opportunity and for granting us safe passage halfway across the world.

Mary Elizabeth was right. It *did* feel like a dream, as if everything was moving in slow motion. A dream where the colors were so rich and vibrant and the experiences so rich in symbolism and meaning that it took your breath away. A dream where the air was so thick, the people so loving, the wildlife so majestic and graceful that it made you never want to visit a zoo again in your life. And the ancestral connectedness flowed like a powerful electrical current from the people of Kenya straight into our souls. My family and I have traveled throughout the world. But finally, Joseph had brought us home.

The sense of community and connectedness was enough to make us slow our step; to look into each other's eyes with a quiet, knowing gaze. To smile a private smile among the four of us—even in the midst of the other families traveling with us who were "ooohing" and "aaaahing" over the lion cubs and the hippos—a smile that came from deep in our souls; that came from knowing that here, in this country where we stood, was where our ancestors had stood; that this is our past and this continent of Africa is the land from whence we came. Yes, in a very real way, it did seem like a dream. It still does.

For father and son—Lonnie and Lonnie Paul—the experience was made even more remarkably symbolic because of Joseph, who had arranged long before our departure for Lonnie Paul and the two other wonderful African American boys on the trip (Andrew Welters and David Cooley) to meet and interact with the African males their age and older. In an elaborate ceremony, Lonnie Paul, Andrew, and David were going to become, in the continent of their ancestors, "junior" Masai warriors, linked inextricably to their heritage and history.

My son, the warrior.

Before the ceremony, Lonnie Paul, Andrew, and David emerged from their tents dressed in full Masai warrior garb—bright red material wrapped around their waists and across their chests; colorful, handmade necklaces adorning their necks; even carrying small wooden spears which they held, right along with the other young warriors who greeted them when they arrived in their village, deep in the bush. Joseph allowed me to come, but only because I insisted. I wanted to film whatever I could and I wanted to *see* whatever they would allow me to see, storing it deep into the recesses of my memory forever. Lonnie, of course, came, too.

As we climbed out of the jeep, Masai warriors young and old surrounded our vehicle. They, too, were dressed in their traditional bright red garb. Some of the older villagers had a dark reddish-looking dye covering their scalps and their legs, a sign of prominence. Many wore headdresses. A young man of about sixteen who wore an elaborate headdress seemed to bond immediately with Lonnie Paul (photo below). I found out later that the headdress he was wearing was made from the mane of a lion he'd killed with a spear to protect his village and the cattle. A mane and mantle of unparalleled distinction, because this young man had shown courage and bravery; but, more important, he had protected the larger community from certain harm.

The men fell into step, a single-file line leading toward their village. As they moved, their steps became more rhythmic. They chanted and hummed a deep, soul-stirring hum. No words were exchanged. There was only the implicit expectation for my son and his two brother-friends to fall into the rhythm and join them, like men and like warriors, in their ritual.

They did.

Through tears, I watched as my son fell into line, moving away from me. *Away* from me. They entered the village while I lingered outside and listened for whatever I could hear of the ceremony. I heard celebratory chanting, feet stamping rhythmically in the dust, drums beating, high-pitched warrior calls. In a few minutes, they emerged.

My son, Lonnie Paul, the young warrior, Masai Mara, Kenya

Something had changed in my son's eyes. His gaze met mine and it was still filled with love. But he did not smile and run to greet me. He lingered with the warriors awhile, then turned to embrace his father, and then Joseph.

His life had been forever changed. He was something larger than his own person. He had suddenly adopted a seriousness of intent; a sense of belonging and, with it, an enhanced inner strength. He didn't speak to me until we returned to the compound.

Only then did he reach out to hold my hand.

The moment I felt his grip, my tears of joy and awakening began their flow.

Later in the trip, on the island of Mombasa, several of us came together, primarily to celebrate the twenty-fifth wedding anniversary of our close friends Tony and Bea Welters. Somehow, Joseph had secretly arranged for a fishing boat—adorned with colorful lights—to take us *away*, on a magical dinner cruise along the Indian Ocean. It was a happy, healing moment for us all. Tony and Bea basked in the moonlight, counting their blessings (like they always do), their souls smiling together at the thought of reaching their twenty-fifth mark.

Bea and I shared smiles, too; smiles that surfaced from deep within our souls. On that day, both of our sons had become young warriors, ready for the world.

Thomas Dortch, Jr., president of the 100 Black Men of America, Inc., is yet another dynamic person I've come to know during this journey of a book. The fact that his and Joseph's views on community converge at one, beautifully enlightened intersection is no accident. It is not a random act or even a lucky coincidence that I was directed to these two beautiful black brothers who share such passionate beliefs—one from a tiny village in Kenya on the other side of the world, the other from a tiny town in South Carolina called Taccoa.

As I've mentioned, I don't believe in coincidence. I believe that God's hand is everywhere.

Listen to Thomas Dortch's story. It is so similar in sequence and theory to Joseph's that it takes my breath away.

In his book, *The Miracles of Mentoring: The Joy of Investing in Our Future*, Dortch describes his birthplace of Taccoa as "a village looking out for its own," a tightly woven community where the adults "were like a security blanket wrapped around us."

And then, the recurring theme of the importance and wisdom of the elders in his life within his community; elders who recognized the vital need for change in a politically and racially charged segregated South.

Says Dortch of his community, "Our elders taught us by example. They came together to make their voices heard politically and economically. . . . They were my inspiration."

So inspiring were his elders that Dortch became president of the student government at Fort Valley State University and later became involved in local and national politics.

Dortch remembers, "I was so filled with pride when I returned years later to that same county in Georgia. . . . Here I was, one of Senator Sam Nunn's chief aides, called in to help resolve racial tensions following a local civil rights demonstration. I brought everything my community had taught me to that negotiating table and celebrated the moment not only as a personal validation, but also as a victory for that whole village who helped raise me."

Sound familiar? It should.

It's the sound of history repeating itself. Different times, different places, and different circumstances, but the deeply felt commitment from these two men who have never even laid eyes on each other resounds loud and clear. They are devoting their lives to "giving back" to their community. Both already have; Joseph Lekuton to his tiny village in Kenya, and Dortch, through his book and his organization, to black youth throughout the United States. I sighed at the thought of it: how beautifully life overlaps itself, in this particular case, with the striking similarities between these two different men who shared the same vision.

Villages Are Beautiful, but It Also Takes Money

Joseph Lekuton and Thomas Dortch are shining examples of how two men from two completely different parts of the world can change and save lives.

Both were selected, inspired, and supported by their elders to achieve the very specific task of saving their own communities (in and of itself, an act that required tremendous vision and foresight from the elders themselves). Both recognized that they could not do it alone. So here we reach the point where all of us should play a role. Herein lies the precise place where we, as individuals, can involve ourselves and re-create communities.

If we are truly committed to the concept of reweaving the beautiful fabric of the black community—the communities we *used* to cherish—we must first acknowledge that this is a task that cannot be performed alone or even in isolated pockets. We must also acknowledge that it cannot be done without significant financial resources. Reliving warm memories costs us nothing. Re-creating some of the shared values and collective wisdom associated with those warm memories and actually redesigning our communities so that they are again cohesive "safety nets" will be staggeringly expensive.

But it can be done.

As a little girl growing up surrounded by all of the beautiful women who were my older sisters, I saw no end to the male suitors who would stop by from time to time to sit on our living room sofa for "courting time." Daddy always insisted that the doors to the living room be left open—*wide* open, not just cracked—when suitors came calling. It was seen as an important rite of passage when Daddy invited one of these young suitors into our kitchen to take a seat at the table. They knew they were in then. Our kitchen table was saved for comfortable, intimate conversations and cherished time together with the family.

I do distinctly remember, though, one *particular* suitor who was then courting my oldest sister, Joann. He'd always come over to visit and talk about lofty literary and political issues. He was the first person I knew who taught me about the concept of "shared community." Even when I was a toddler, wearing pigtails and Buster Browns, I felt the electricity in the air whenever he paid us a visit. Thus, Daddy adored him.

Dr. Claud Anderson, who graduated from our living room couch to our kitchen table faster than the speed of sound, is widely recognized today as one of the country's most innovative African American thinkers. In one of his books, *Powernomics: The National Plan to Empower Black America*, he speaks about community, just as he did that day in our kitchen decades ago.

This time, though, as we settled in to talk about black communities for the purpose of my book, we sat at Joann and Claud's kitchen table. And this time, as a grown woman rather than a toddler, I not only understood Claud's philosophies; for the most part, I embraced them.

I read his books with relish; I listen to his lectures and attend his public appearances with pride.

"Within our national network, we must build competitive communities that contain social, political, economic, religious, educational, and geographic assets that act as foundations of power," he says in *Powernomics*, ideas that he reiterates at the kitchen table.

"Blacks don't even realize what tremendous wealth we have accumulated over the years," he says. "And the tragedy is that we let our own wealth slip out of our hands so quickly—many, many billions of dollars a year—that *our own money* barely has a chance to bounce even *once* in our own community."

His theory is that if we strategically rebuild functional black communities so that our cumulative wealth can become self-contained, we can economically empower ourselves in a way that we never have before. He also strongly believes that integration was one of the worst things that has happened to black America.

"Integration actually turned out to be a form of deliberate, debilitating fragmentation," he says, more in disappointment than despair.

"Black folks are *still* celebrating the fact that the black race has been 'integrated,' " he says. "Integration didn't bring our communities closer together. It divided us and took us further apart. And because of that, we no longer have common interests. Everybody's out to get their own.

"Once you rebuild a community, you learn how to create ways of developing alternative economic structures inside the community, where your money, your values, and your trust stay with the group at large," Claud says.

Money. Values. Trust. Self-determination: all vitally important threads that *have* to be woven ever so tightly together as we re-weave the unraveling threads of the black community.

"The majority of black Americans live in impoverished black neighborhoods and spend approximately 95 percent of their annual disposable income with people who live outside of the neighborhood," Claud says in his book. "They spend only five percent of their disposable income in black neighborhoods. They spend three percent with non-black-owned businesses that are located in black neighborhoods but whose owners live outside of black neighborhoods."

He is exactly right.

He continues: "Thus, only two percent of black America's disposable income is spent in black-owned businesses in black neighborhoods. It is impossible for any large population or neighborhood to be self-sufficient on only two percent of its own income. By spending its disposable income in other groups' businesses and communities," he says, "black America impoverishes itself and impedes the growth of its own functional communities."

Here are the things we need to re-create if we are to rebuild our communities: *Shared* wealth. *Shared* values. *Shared* vision. "Buy-in" from *everyone* is required, which, in most cases, will necessitate a dramatic change in our thinking, our spending habits, our undaunted determination, and our ability to move beyond—or above—the stability of our own creature comforts.

In another of his best-selling books, *Black Labor, White Wealth,* Claud reminds us that cohesion and commitment are essential, particularly in our quest for increased economic power.

"In the founding years of this nation," he writes in *Black Labor*, "European whites built their dreams of becoming a wealthy aristocracy . . . on the backs of black slaves.

"The collective power and resources of many people, nations, religions, and organizations were aligned and concertedly used to exploit blacks. This strategy illustrates that group power requires general agreement among the participating members on a core issue, but power evolves from the group's collective motives and goals."

His message rings as true today as it did four decades ago, sitting at our kitchen table.

But when will we stop long enough to listen?

When we begin to rebuild communities, it becomes possible to re-create the collective values and shared principles that once bound black families together; the values that were so carefully passed down to me, which I now pass down to my own children. The values and principles, yes, I can pass down to my children. But my children—and yours—will never know the joys, the sense of safety and belonging, or the sense of being a part of something larger than themselves unless we decide to re-create it together. If we choose to turn our backs on our own rich past and the beauty of what once was a strong and vibrant collective culture, our children will not have to turn to their science books to figure out Charles Darwin's theory of survival of the fittest. No, they'll experience it firsthand: those species who are able to retain—and pass along to successive generations—the most adaptable traits for survival will be the ones who'll flourish. All other species and subspecies, because of their inability to adapt to changing environments, gradually give way to extinction.

Although I am usually not given to drama, I *am always* given to sharing what I think is the truth: if we do not become more adaptable, we will, put simply, become extinct.

What we need to do is this: let's get about the task of *valuing and validating our men again—the fathers of our children. We must return the black father and the African American male back to his mantel, return to*

the values and visions we once shared, and rekindle the familial flame that
is burning dangerously low. A slow and arduous task.

But it can be done.

An old African American proverb says it best by placing far more value on the collective, *aggregate* result than on any one individual person or thing: *"Little flakes make de deepest snow."*

Before it's too late, let's become snowmakers. Let's build mountains and more mountains of snow. Each individual flake that falls builds our mountain higher and higher. I like the way Ella Fitzgerald says it: "Let it snow, let it snow, let it snow!"

———◆———

A closing quote by Kenneth C. Edelin,
urging us toward a more collective community:

"While it may take a village to raise a child,
it takes responsible and caring adults
to make a nurturing village."

———◆———

So let's raise our glasses *and* our spirits in a toast, if you will—to snowflakes and villages.

6.

THE MIRACLE
OF MENTORING

OUTSTRETCH YOUR HAND! SAVE A LIFE!

The black community has traditionally taken care of its own. As a natural extension of the previous chapter on shared communities comes the equally important collective task of keeping those extended familial communities focused, forward-looking, and uplifted.

Because the structure of the black family unit has shifted so dramatically over the years, it becomes imperative for us to inspire and uplift *all* families—particularly those without a father figure in the house or a paternal presence in their lives.

That's where mentoring comes in.

There are hundreds of African American organizations whose mission it is to provide structure, substance, and an enhanced sense of self-esteem to those young people who are in need of a more focused vision. This chapter is written to celebrate mentors everywhere, the ones who do their work quietly, under a cloak of modesty, as well as the ones who sing a song of faith with loud, clear voices for the world to hear. But it is also an invitation to people everywhere to get involved.

We've already discussed the need for re-creating our communities.

Now comes the task of bolstering and buttressing those individuals within our communities who need that extra helping hand, that inviting, outstretched hand.

————◆————

"My mother and father had divorced shortly after my birth. As the years rolled by, however, I did not have the chance to turn into the pitiful little black boy who had been abandoned by his father. There was a reason: other men showed up. They were warm, honest (at least as far as my eyes could see) and big-hearted. They were the good black men in the shadows, the men who taught me right from wrong, who taught me how to behave, who told me, by their very actions, that they expected me to do good things in life."

—WIL HAYGOOD, IN *UNDERGROUND DADS*

————◆————

My own father is a good example.

I don't think my father really *had* a father to speak of. I know virtually nothing about my father's childhood or his upbringing. He was always extremely private and protective of his childhood memories, and to this day, I respect that. We know virtually nothing about Daddy's life before us. It's as though *he* didn't exist before *we* did. And the information that we have about his childhood is splattered and splotched; a patchwork of information gathered over the years that creates a fragmented framework of truths and half-truths about Daddy's life before we came along. As for Daddy's father, he was a phantom, a ghost, not even a wisp of a memory or the vestige of a dream.

But yet and still, my father was the king of the Clark castle; he was the dark, handsome prince who kept his family safe. I've asked myself a thousand times:

How did this man who was my father, who had no father to speak of, transform himself into one of the most gracious and loving men I've ever known? What was it that made him so solid and self-assured as a father and a husband when he had no models from which to draw or on whom he could pattern himself? How could it be that he was always there to protect me from those ugly three-headed monsters that used to hide under my bed when *he himself, as a child, must have struggled with a similarly overactive imagination—probably valiantly and, perhaps tragically, alone?*

And while these questions will live forever unanswered in my mind, this much I know for sure: there must have been a handful of positive father figures in Daddy's life—guardian angels, if you will—who helped him along the way.

Maybe it was the pastor of his church. Or a neighbor down the road. Maybe a distant relative, or the barber down the block.

Whoever it was, it is clear to me that Daddy was guided by the hand of God to take the "Good Father" route because he knew, either instinctively or from personal experience, that the "Bad Father" route was one that he'd never choose to impose upon his own children, if he ever had any.

Maybe he gave so much love and light to us, his children, *precisely* because he received so little during his own childhood. I don't know. I only can send silent prayers of thanks to those faceless men (and women) who did act as role models for him when he was a boy, consciously or unconsciously. My guess is that these people, these guardian angels, these miraculous mentors, probably saved my father's life. And if you look for such angels, you'll see them there. Sitting beside you in church or walking ahead of you when you cross the street. Lighting on your shoulder as you merge onto Route 66. Directing your steps away from certain danger and despair. That is what angels do. I do believe they saved my father's life as a child.

And because they saved his, they saved mine.

I know of some angels whom you can reach out and touch. They cry when they're sad and bleed when they're hurt. I suppose I should call them human beings who are angels. They are the mentors—seen and unseen—who offer our African American children hope and promise. They work hard to help transform mediocre men into miraculous fathers, even though they don't bill themselves as angels, I'm sure.

But that is precisely what they are.

They enrich lives, and, in many cases, they save them. They extend an open hand to those African American youth who need to feel the certainty of a strong grip to pull them back from the brink of despair and loneliness and confusion.

Particularly for African American youth who are looking not only to be good or better citizens, but good or better people; or for black fathers who simply need a guiding hand, leaning on a mentor is one answer. It is the salve that helps the healing process begin and the soothing balm that encourages new growth, directly from the root.

Thomas Dortch, whom I mentioned earlier as being the inspiring and inspired national president of the 100 Black Men of America, Inc., said this to me during a recent conversation: "Mentors change lives,

Many generations celebrated the Million Man March

many times in ways that they themselves don't even recognize or appreciate."

How very, very true. I think of Daddy again, and I silently thank the faceless mentors whom I'll never know who offered him a helping hand.

Says Dortch, "Ultimately, we want to pass down a certain part of ourselves to future generations, through our own children, through the children we mentor. . . . The important thing is to be clear with yourself about what it is that you value enough in your own character that you want to encourage in the characters of young people."

Be clear, Dortch warns.

Because, as both my parents used to say and as I still strongly believe, you never know how your actions can influence a young person's life.

You never know who it is or what will be said that might lighten a spirit or redirect the course of a young person's life.

How to Find Faith in the Fathers Who Are Struggling

Dortch's organization works with thousands of African American youth across the United States, both male and female. For black fathers who remain in the home with their families, trying (and many times struggling) to provide for and protect their wives and children while, at the same time, beating back the ugly obstacles of prejudice and pain, there is also relief. Relief that leaves their pride—as men and as fathers—intact. But it is a difficult ball to balance, says Dortch.

"With many of the families we work with, the father is a part of the household," he says. "In this case, we provide extensive mentor training and orientation to assure that our mentors do nothing to minimize or undermine the father's role within the family."

I'm praying and thanking God for people like Thomas Dortch as he speaks into the phone. They'll never know the extent of the good that they actually do. But on this issue—mentoring males when the father remains at home—Dortch makes himself clear.

"We don't want to be substitute fathers," he says. "And we don't ever want to put the father in the position of feeling embarrassed or undervalued in his role at home. . . . We are very conscientious about walking that fine line between what a black father can provide for his children and what a mentor can provide to his mentee. And when the father is at home, we don't run away from our responsibility to the family. We just carefully modify it to preserve the dignity of the father."

So here's the beauty of a mentoring relationship, as I see it, with a young black male whose father is living at home, as well as the gentle guidance I want to offer the African American child: to the extent that it is hurtful or stands in the way of your progress, try with all your heart to dissolve the particles of pride that prevent you from getting the most that you possibly can from both your father and your mentor, because what they are offering you are different and distinct benefits. The father of the family is offering you (or trying his level best to offer you) his presence and his strength, of which he may have precious little at this particular moment in his life. The mentor is offering you encouragement, guidance, structured time, and an opportunity to establish a relationship with a black male figure outside of your family based on mutual trust and respect.

My advice: take it all! Because we know too well that so many of our young black children are overwhelmed and paralyzed by feelings of confusion, anger, disenfranchisement, and fear. Those were the feelings that my own father probably wore wrapped around his shoulders when he was a little boy, but somewhere along the line, something was said or done that absolutely turned his life around. And, most important, he must have accepted and received it with grace and dignity. Which is what we should be offering our children. And encouraging them to take it.

Celebrating the Unsung Surrogates

Recently, I shared a cup of coffee in a downtown hotel with a man named LeRoy Potts, Sr.

Potts—a neat, impassioned man who, for some reason, reminded me of my own father—heads an organization in Philadelphia called the Fathering Program. His program offers a very specific, highly specialized, twelve-week course on "fathering" to men (predominantly African American) who have lost their way and are struggling hard to get back on track.

The pamphlet he hands me across the table describes the program as one offering "free parent education and support for men who want to improve their relationship and involvement with their children."

I study the pamphlet thoughtfully, happy to be in the presence of this deliberate and purposeful man who reminds me of Daddy and so thoroughly enriches and redirects the lives of young African American fathers.

Although he probably won't admit it, because of his quiet humility, Potts's program, like Dortch's, saves lives by *enriching* lives.

Potts describes himself as a "hands-on" kind of a guy.

"I travel throughout Philly just about every day," he says over coffee, "posting flyers about the program, visiting schools, stopping to talk with any young black male I can find who might benefit from participating in my program."

There's been many a time, he explains with dancing eyes, when he's walked right up to a group of young black men standing on a street corner, introduced himself, engaged them in conversation to see if any of them happened to be fathers who need a helping hand, and offered them that helping hand, right then and there. Others, he says, are sent to him by county or state authorities.

"I do a lot of outreach to black males who are struggling to be good fathers," he says, "but many of the people who come into my program are captive audiences because they are being required by the state to participate; these are the fathers in drug and alcohol programs, fathers who have just been released from prison and may not have ever even *met* their children (much less have had an opportunity to develop a relationship with them), fathers who are simply trying to get to know their children again and adjust to life 'outside,' either in halfway houses or work-release programs. These men are struggling hard and trying to balance a lot in their lives—including the challenge of learning (or relearning) the task of being a good father," Potts says.

He sips at the coffee that is the color of my father's complexion.

"Most of the men we treat are men who grew up fatherless themselves," Potts observes.

I think of my own father. Dark storm clouds form in the back of my mind as I imagine Daddy as the fatherless, lonely child he might have been.

"Somehow, these men think that because *they* grew up without fathers and they were able to, as they say, 'survive,' that their children should be able to survive as well. They think that growing up without a father somehow made them stronger; better able to cope; better able to survive the streets," he says with a sad smile. "This, we all know, is a fallacy.

"On the other hand," he says, "many of the men who participate in our program are fully, vitally, and painfully aware that they have short-changed their children by not being there for them; by being imprisoned or addicted to drugs or living on the streets.

"Strangely enough," he says, "the ones who recognize their weakness and the pain that they've caused themselves and their families are the ones who want the most to be helped and guided. These are the men who come out of the program after twelve weeks and give me the ultimate compliment by saying, 'Twelve weeks isn't long enough for a program like this! There's so much more I think I could learn!' "

What Potts's Fathering Program does is this:

- Provides counseling and out-patient services to fathers who are in distress
- Offers on-site child care by licensed social workers for the children of every participating father (it is required that the children spend at least part of the program at the center, with their fathers, for purposes of evaluation and interactive father-child discussions)
- Offers courses and specific training in fathering techniques and guidance on how these fathers can re-introduce and re-assimilate themselves back into society
- Offers hope, guidance, and an outstretched helping hand to those who need it most

"While the dads are in session with us," Potts explains, "we either have a social worker or a certified child-care worker who watches their children, plays with them, and, most important, engages them in conversation."

The program is well coordinated enough, Potts explains, so that the social worker or child-care provider is always "prepped" about the specific issues that the counselors are discussing with the fathers in a separate part of the building, so that when father and child are brought together for discussion, productive father-child interaction can take place in a controlled environment.

"For example," Potts explains, "after a support session with the fathers on the importance of spending 'quality time' with their children or on the issue of the importance of financial responsibility, we might bring in the children and ask them, 'If you had one wish that only your daddy could make come true, what would it be?'

"Initially, the kids will always respond with something like, 'I'd like for my daddy to buy me that new toy I saw on TV; the one that all the kids at school have except for me!' "

He explains how they quickly and expertly maneuver around a child's material desires:

"When this happens, we immediately rephrase the question and say, 'Okay, say there's no money involved at all. No toys. No new gizmos. . . . *Now*, what would you like most from your dad?' "

The answer from the children, invariably, has to do with time. Quality time.

"Once the father hears their child tell them, in a controlled environment, that all they really want to do is spend time with them, the dynamics begin to change dramatically. We can create an environment for the father where he does not feel inadequate or incapable of providing for his child; an environment that doesn't assign blame or point fingers," he says softly. "That way, the father is more easily accepting [of] what his child says, and the child doesn't feel threatened or intimidated by saying it," Potts explains.

"But there's always that balance: it's a challenge to help these fathers understand that money management and providing for their children to the extent that they can is essential, but there are things they can provide that their children want and need that don't cost a cent."

What kinds of things? I ask. He ticks them off with as much ease as we could, conceivably, provide them:

- A walk down the street
- A game of one-on-one at the local basketball hoops
- A visit to the zoo or a picnic in the park
- A visit with the child's teacher to see how he's doing in school
- A smile; an embrace

What the Fathering Program has done is to empower the fathers to be mentors to their own children. It teaches them how to re-introduce themselves into their children's lives. It offers the fathers themselves a chance to breathe; to regroup; to allow themselves the luxury of letting others who can, provide help, guidance, and an outstretched hand.

People like Potts and Dortch are our guardian angels, providing light where there was only darkness. Providing smiles where there were only tears. Pulling us together again to teach us how to provide hope and happiness to those who need it most.

Each One, Teach One

Miracles never cease. Nor do the benefits of mentoring.

It was Vincent Mathews, a man whose interview appears earlier in this book, who reminded me of the value of communal mentoring; of the concept of "each one, teach one" as the primary concept that will sew the fabric of our black families together again.

In addition to being a mentor, pastor, author, and father of seven, Mathews is a lover of philosophy. His theory is that, in order to mentor effectively, we must adopt the philosophy of the Fulani people of Nigeria. Here is the philosophical contrast he provides.

"The French philosopher Descartes coined the phrase, 'I think, therefore I am,' " Mathews begins slowly.

"The Western world we live in is filled with 'I, I, I,' and 'I think' this, and 'I think' that."

True. True.

"Well, I don't buy it," he says definitively; dismissively. I look around to see if it's me he's dismissing. He's not. He's only dismissing the selfishness that we, as a people, display as proudly as we display our new cars and fancy homes.

"When I talk to young people who need guidance, or to people who are going to be acting in some capacity as mentors, I tell them to remember the philosophy of the Fulani people, which is this," he says.

I sit up and take note. The man is ready to preach.

"This is the philosophy of the Fulani," he says, clearing his throat:

"I am because *we* are. And since *we* are, therefore, *I am*."

How wonderfully, refreshingly, totally different than this Western world's egocentric, self-driven, "I've got mine now you better get yours" philosophy. It's not really about "I" or "me" at all. It's about "us."

Because it has to be. The alternative is frightening.

Mathews continues: "This African concept affirms that we are all part of a larger continuum, and that each one must teach one if we are to survive as a people.

"When I talk to the young people I mentor, I tell them, in no uncertain terms, 'Everything I am is because of what somebody before me was, and I'm standing on their shoulders. I might not have known them, but I know that they taught, inspired, and led all of those people who came before me, and that not only gives me tremendous strength—but it should give you the same amount of strength,' " he says in a burst of energy, as if he's just finishing . . . and winning . . . the fifty-yard dash.

"This is what we should be teaching the young African American children that we're mentoring: the fact that they are not alone; and more than that, their place in the universe dictates that they *never* will be alone, or else our entire race and our entire culture is in jeopardy."

Each one, teach one: Father to child. Child to father. Mentor to mentee. All with a sense of dignity and grace.

Another young man whom my Holy Father has led me to during the writing of my book is named Mishala Muhammad. He, too, is a mentor, in more ways than one.

"One of the main goals of my fraternity, Alpha Phi Alpha," Muhammad explains, "is to mentor young black men and to save them, sometimes from themselves."

He goes on to explain that his fraternity "has leadership conferences on a regular basis. We mentor black males from the ninth grade through their senior year in high school, then provide them scholarships to colleges and universities. Many of these young people," he says, "would never have had a chance if we hadn't stepped up to the plate."

Stepping up to the plate *should be* easy enough, I think to myself. Especially at a time in our history when we're sending more young black men to the state penn than to Penn State. Why can't every one of us do what Mishala and other black fraternities and organizations are doing? What is it that's stopping us?

In addition to teaching and inspiring (Mishala also works with LeRoy Potts in the Fathering Program), he is a man who wants to learn. He wants to learn how to do things the right way before he enters into the world of fatherhood. Mishala, too, needs a mentor. Fortunately for him, he's already had many in his life.

Says Mishala, "I am not married and I am not a father. I would love to be a father and I know well all the responsibilities that come with it; responsibilities that I have learned from my own father and grandfather, and responsibilities that I now teach to other fathers." He pauses thoughtfully.

"I work with my brothers who are fathers who are facing huge obstacles in their lives," he goes on. "Fathers who are estranged from their children, who are struggling with substance abuse; who are trying hard to keep their relationship with their families alive.

"And, because of the values my parents instilled in me as I was being raised, I've made the conscious decision not to become a father until I know everything that *should* be right *is* right: I believe with all my heart and soul that a family must start with a man and a wife; then the children come after that—in that order. . . . For the sake of society, for the sake of the fabric of the black family, and remembering the lessons that I was taught as a child, I'll know when the time is right," he says with conviction.

"I need to continue to learn, though; to continue being taught by other black fathers who are doing it the right way, so that when the time comes for me, I'll be able to do it right, too.

"At this point in my life," he says, "I refuse to perpetuate this destructive cycle that doesn't value the dignity of black fathers and their relationships with their families. I haven't found a mate yet who I want to spend the rest of my life with, so my cycle of fatherhood has not yet begun," he says with clarity and conviction.

"But this is by my own choice and my own design," he explains.

"I am a teacher to my brothers, yes. But I am still looking to be taught as well."

Mishala is one of many thousands of men who are active, conscientious members of historic black fraternities and who act as mentors to black youth. It is these "brothers" in these fraternal orders who come together with the single, collective goal of helping their younger brothers out. For decades, black fraternities (and sororities) have been a vital, visible component of the community, as well as a source of pride and strength to young men (and women) who need an extended hand to pull them up—or away—from the ravages of racism and a world where alienation and isolation are commonplace. To every fraternity brother—and sorority sister—who ever offered a hand, an idea, a vision, a visit to our young black men and women who are trying to find their way, I thank you. You are proud brothers, all of you. Mentors who make a difference in people's lives. Keep doing what you're doing. Keep giving our young people something—and someone—to look up to.

Another brilliant black mentor was a man named George Washington Carver. Although Carver never married, he considered Tuskegee Institute in Alabama, where he taught for forty-seven years, to be his "surrogate family." His students were his children, and he pulled them under his wing protectively. He was clearly their shining mentor, as bright as the North Star. He considered himself—because he characterized it in his own words—their "father."

In a letter to the representative of the Class of 1922, Carver writes,

Mr. L. Robinson:

I wish to express through you to each member of the Senior class my deep appreciation for the fountain pen you so kindly and thoughtfully gave me at Christmas.

The gift, like all the others, is characterized by simplicity and thoughtfulness, which I hope each member will make the slogan of their lives.

As your father, it is needless for me to keep saying, I hope, exception for emphasis, that each one of my children will rise to the full height of your possibilities, which means the possession of these eight cardinal virtues which constitutes a lady or a gentleman:

1st. Be clean both inside and outside.

2nd. Who neither looks up to the rich or down to the poor.

3rd. Who loses, if need be, without squealing.

4th. Who wins without bragging.

5th. Who is always considerate of women, children and old people.

6th. Who is too brave to lie.

7th. Who is too generous to cheat.

8th. Who takes his share of the world and lets other people have theirs.

May God help you carry out these eight cardinal virtues and peace and prosperity be yours through life.

Carver's "eight cardinal virtues" speak to us with as much urgency today as they did when he wrote the letter in 1922. Perhaps more. Wouldn't we be wise to listen, to pass it on to our own progeny?

Another touching story from an African American male
who played the role of father and mentor to a child
who was not his own:

"My nephew Charles was my heart. I was his uncle, almost his father, even if only for the day, the weekend, the week or summers we were together. . . . His skin was darker than ours at the same time that it was more brilliant. He shone. His was a preternatural blackness dedicated to the light. His round face was like a thundercloud with the lightning of his eyes and teeth constantly flashing inside it.

"I loved that boy better than my life. . . .

"When his mother was pregnant with him, I used to sit by

A vital, visual, paternal presence is mandatory for all black children

her and touch her stomach and read to him inside her womb. . . . By the time Charles was born, his father was back on heroin. My brother tried many times to save himself, to heal, to redeem himself, and no one knows better than I do that he was born into a world of trouble. And maybe the reason I loved his son so much was that I loved my brother, and I hoped I could redeem him if I could help redeem them."

—DON BELTON,

AUTHOR OF *VOODOO FOR CHARLES*

To all who participated in this chapter, who advanced their unique and generous solutions to the challenges of mentoring, you are our faithful fathers. Praise to you for the promise of your presence.

7.

MOVING FORWARD
BY LOOKING BACK

LEARNING FROM THOSE
WHO CAME BEFORE US

———◆———

"Your ancestors took the lash, the branding iron,
humiliations, and oppression because one day they
believed you would come along to flesh out the dream."
—MAYA ANGELOU

Many times I have said in the pages of this book that looking *back* at the wisdom of our forefathers will help us move forward as a people. This chapter shines a glowing spotlight on those who came before us; on the dignity and grace they struggled to maintain as faithful fathers, despite the brutal bumps and "the branding iron" to which Maya Angelou refers that tried to break their spirits but couldn't. It is a chapter that celebrates and recognizes the forefathers who fought for their children, and whose children's children fought for us. In present and future generations, our determination must not wane. Because the battle is not yet over. It's really only just begun.

———◆———

"If we are lucky and our fathers are still with us, we owe it to ourselves to take them down from the pedestal and talk to them about their lives. I don't mean just listening to them tell of playful reminiscences. I mean their experiences and encounters. This may require a gentle nudge or even a hard push. But it's important because they are not only our fathers. They are our elders. And their past can serve as our signpost for the future."

—EARL OFARI HUTCHINSON,

FROM *BLACK FATHERHOOD:*

THE GUIDE TO BLACK MALE PARENTING

———◆———

I have always reveled in and revered the connective generational thread that weaves families together over time. For me, it has provided an endless source of comfort and stability. It connects to my past, helps me make sense of my present, and guides me as I step into the future.

———◆———

"We, today, stand on the shoulders of our predecessors who
have gone before us. We, as their successors,
must catch the torch of freedom and liberty
passed on to us by our ancestors."

—BENJAMIN MAYS, EDUCATOR

———◆———

The "torch" to which Mays refers is one we all must pass to our own children, one we can never allow to be extinguished. It is the torch of connectedness and collective consciousness. It is a torch that I, for one, am proud to carry.

Before he died, I was blessed to have seen my father develop a close and loving relationship with my son, Lonnie Paul. I'd watch the two of them fishing together or lying outside on a blanket in the sun, enjoying their intergenerational time together.

The sight would fill my heart with such joy that, quite often, I could not find the words to speak. I wouldn't have wanted to speak anyway; these were clearly their grandfather-grandson moments, not to be disturbed. Only to be cherished.

"Daddy Jim" and Lonnie Paul spending quality time together

As black families struggle to gird themselves more mightily with the armor of our forefathers, it is important to realize the value of preserving not only the wisdom of earlier generations, but to re-create the strength and undying tenacity of those earlier generations as well, passing them down to our own children. Parents—fathers and mothers alike—would do well to actively preserve and instill the memory of their forefathers into the lives of their children.

My Father's Garden

Vincent Mathews, the author-motivator-preacher-father I introduced earlier in this book, provides a living, breathing model of how black families should be consciously working to weave together the beautiful, multi-generational fabric of today's black family.

Says Mathews, "There are four living generations of fathers that I can share with my children."

And share them he does.

"I take my children to visit their great-grandfather all the time," Mathews says, "and as a result, there is a very, very strong bond between them—just as there is a strong bond between every generation of my family, especially amongst the men."

The black men. The standard-bearers. The fathers. The proud patriarchs, through whose veins flow the continuation of the family name; who cement the family's very existence. Mathews reminds me that his tight-knit family bonds didn't create themselves randomly or by accident. He worked hard at creating the resin that binds his multigenerational family together. This achievement did not happen by mistake. It is an intentional and deliberate act of love, by his own admission. He shares the story of how the generations of his family unfolded:

"My grandfather moved to Detroit from Texas many, many years ago," he says.

As if reading my mind and anticipating my next question, he leaps forward. "But there is a story behind how and why my grandfather ended up in Detroit.

"My grandfather used to work in a Texas sawmill. During that time, if the overseer of the mill didn't like what he saw some of the blacks doing, he'd come up to them and hit them hard with a belt."

His emphasis on the word "hard" makes me flinch.

"Well, my grandfather never created a moment's worth of trouble for anyone, so on the day the foreman came up to him and, for no reason in the world, lifted the belt to my grandfather as if he were about to aim that thick buckle right at his face, my grandfather looked him straight in the eye and said, 'If you swing that thing at *me*, I can guarantee you won't be living tomorrow to see the light of day.' And the overseer walked away. Just like that."

Just like that sounded too simple. Too simple during a time when black men couldn't get away with threatening a white man in public.

"Well, nothing actually happened between my grandfather and his overseer *then*—on that actual day," says Mathews.

I knew it would have been too simple. Things are always so complicated and convoluted for a black man who is trying mightily to preserve his dignity and keep his family intact. So Mathews continues:

"That same night, though, my grandfather and his family heard that the foreman and a large group of other angry white men were planning on 'getting him' real soon. Whether 'get him' meant beating him, lynching him, or killing him, my grandfather didn't stay around long enough to find out. He knew he had to get out of town, which is exactly what he did."

I wondered as he was talking how many black men's lives and how many black families had been destroyed, broken up, beaten back, and fragmented—particularly during that time—by the threats of an angry mob or even a simple cross word exchanged between a Negro man and a white man.

"My grandfather left his entire family—he had two children and a wife. He left his family and came to Detroit."

The wonderful story of northern migration in all of its splendid colors, I think cynically. How many other black men were forced to make that same involuntary trek?

"He was homeless for a while, but then he found work. He worked two jobs and finally made enough money to bring his wife and children to Detroit. He might have been run out of town, but he set down stakes in Detroit, brought his family back together around him, and started his life all over."

My eyes sting in anger at the thought of a grown man with two children and a wife having to start his life all over because of one "bad day" at the sawmill. I pray for God to remove the bitterness in my heart in the same way He's so beautifully removed the bitterness from the heart of my son, Lonnie Paul.

"He bought a nice plot of land, built himself a solid, pretty brick house, and put a garden out back," Mathews says.

Proud grandson. Sharing his generational memories.

"That's one of the reasons I take my children to visit as often as I do. Not only do we all live in the same area, but there are some tough lessons about life and about a man's will and determination that my children can learn by looking at their great-grandfather. And I do everything I can to make sure that those generational lessons are shared and passed down. Just about every weekend, my children spend time with their great-grandfather, working in his garden and talking about old times. It's something that can never be duplicated."

Mathews's generational story continues to unfold:

"I also let my children know that not only is their great-grandfather a great man, but their grandfather is, too."

He describes his father as a man of tremendous pride and determination. But he, too, suddenly, fell down on his luck.

"I remember when my father was laid off," says Mathews. "Even as a young boy, I remember him being laid off for *a long time*—not just for a few weeks, but for *months*," he recalls.

And here it comes, I think, waiting expectantly for him to continue—a shining ray of hope and determination out of the ashes of a story about despair. Mathews, as always, delivers on his promise to deliver optimism in an otherwise dark, pessimistic world.

"As I look at the generations of men in my family, from my grandfather to my father, all I see is strength. Because strength emerges most dramatically out of dark, dismal situations. The common characteristics that exist between and within the generations of the fathers in my family is definitely *strength* and *sacrifice*."

He continues, "Now that I reflect back on my father, I realize how much he sacrificed for us, his children. When I was a boy, I used to look at my father and just figure he was a man who just didn't eat much. It took me years to realize that, particularly during those lean years when he was unemployed, my father didn't eat so that his children could."

The silver lining in the cloud. If it is to be found at all, this man named Vincent Mathews will find it.

"We all used to look at each other after we'd had dinner and were sitting around with our stomachs full and say, 'Man, for a grown adult, Dad sure is a light eater!' I didn't realize then that he was leaving it all for his children and his wife. He just refused to let us go without. And he obviously picked up this generational trait from his own father, because my grandfather is exactly the same way. Determined. Ready to sacrifice for his family. Focused. Brave."

I admire Mathews's ability to draw living parallels between the genera-

tions in his life; admire him even more that he is willing and able to share these real-life generational parallels with his children so that they can see this continuity with their own eyes, feel its comfort within their own souls.

"Well, my father loved to garden, too, when we were small," he recalls lovingly. "I'd spend hours in my father's and, later, my grandfather's gardens, helping them prune and weed and till the soil."

His father's and his grandfather's gardens provide the living roots that bind his family together in strength and in love. Pretty spectacular, I think.

"Today, my own children love to garden with their grandfather. Today, of course, his gardening is just a hobby. But back when I was small, it was probably what helped save our lives. When my father wasn't working and there was NO money coming in, I remember my grandfather would be out there in that yard, pruning those plants and tilling that soil. There were many days when we'd have tomatoes, squash, and cucumber for dinner, and I didn't even think to ask, 'Where's *the meat?*' because I was just so happy and proud that we'd provided our own dinner from our own garden.

"I was proud that all of us—spanning the generations—actively participated in ensuring the survival of our family. And one way we did it was through my father's and grandfather's gardens."

Make no mistake about it, Vincent Mathews has already begun the task of raising an entirely new generation of gardeners; these gardeners who are his sons, who are still fortunate enough to enrich the soil for their own children yet to come.

If that's not a story about roots and about laying a strong foundation for our families and about sharing the wisdom of successive generations, then I don't know what is.

Fortunately, there are many young African Americans who have grown strong, spiritually and emotionally, from having many paternal "roots" grow in their father's gardens; the garden that is Vincent Mathews's.

The beauty of turning to our extended family and to the memory of those who came before us is that within the black family unit, there are so *many* roots to nurture, all of which coexist in a harmony that God Himself created—but that *we* have to work hard at pruning.

Time becomes even more precious when it's being shared between the generations

It was a brilliant young black man named David A. Cooley who recognized, while sitting down with me for an interview, that *that* particular day was his actual birthday. Like any teenager, I'm sure there were other things he would have rather been doing, but there he sat in my sunroom, calmly and patiently, reflecting on the fathers in his family. A deeply spiritual young man with a heart the size of the state of Montana, David began by recognizing the bountiful blessings in his life. Not only was it his birthday, but it was a day to reflect on the fathers in his life, those fathers who keep him firmly anchored to his past and solidly connected to his future. His paternal soil is rich and varied.

In his own words:

Many Fathers, Many Blessings

I am very blessed to have many fathers in my life.

The myth that many young black men don't have solid fathers in their lives, for me anyway, is just not true. My [maternal] grandfather, Junius Cooley, who I call "Papa," is alive and well—and he plays a very important role in my life. He's seventy-four years old, but he looks like he's forty.

I know Papa will do anything for me. He'd step in front of a truck to save my life. I spent the first eight years of my life living under his roof. He takes me to church. We run errands together. He gives me money and gifts, even when I don't need it. He teaches me about life and tells me about the days when he was young, and I really, really learn a lot from that. I visit him all the time, because we're very close—geographically and spiritually. I wouldn't be who I am today without the influence and presence of my grandfather, Junius Cooley.

I know this might sound kind of corny or unrealistic, but Papa is there for me whenever I need him. I know for a fact that lots of other teenagers just don't have that kind of relationship with their grandfathers. It's just not something you see with a lot of high school students, especially African American boys. It kind of makes it all the more special.

My stepfather is another important "father" in my life. He's been an important part of my life since I was two and a half years old, and together, he, my mom, Val, and my two brothers, Michael and Marvin, are a happy black family living under the same roof. Although my parents are no longer together, my biological father loves me very, very much and our relationship has even improved tremendously in the last few years, as I've moved into being a teenager. When I was younger, my stepfather and I used to have quite a difficult

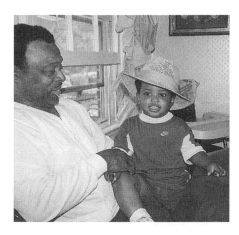

Junius Cooley with his grandson, David

time. We'd argue and disagree, especially on vacations and during school breaks. But it was two things that helped strengthen our relationship. The first was my closer relationship with God, which grew stronger and stronger beginning when I was about five years old, when I accepted the Lord into my heart. The second factor was my mother. It hurt me to see her get upset when my stepfather and I argued. She is the anchor in my life, and I realized that what I was doing—arguing with my stepfather—wasn't really fair to her at all. It hurt her very much. So I really tried hard to work at being a better person. And my stepfather, Marvin, tried harder, too. Now, things are much, much better between us. Even though we still have our problems, I love him very much.

My biological father is a man I love very, very much. I guess it's the unique way that only a biological father and son can love each other. We share the same blood. I am the spitting image of him, and I can see it more and more each day. I've had my problems with him, of course—just like I've had ups and downs with my stepdad, too, but it took me a long time to realize that that's natural. Now, we get along much, much better than we used to. I see him almost every weekend, because he lives close in the area, too.

What I love most about my father is that he tries hard to find fun things for us to do together—father-son activities that might sound simple or boring to others, but that mean so much to us both. When we get together on the weekends, we enjoy each other's company. That's because he really tries hard to make sure we spend meaningful time together on the weekends, and now that I'm old enough to realize what he's been trying to do all the time, I love him even more. Sure, we have our differences, too, but just because he and my mom are no longer together, he hasn't stopped loving me.

Out of all of this, I realize a lot of things. One is that divorce is an ugly thing. I know this personally because I've seen the way it's really screwed up a lot of my friends—especially those who don't have fathers or grandfathers who care enough to try to stick around after the breakup. Divorce can be pretty painful, not just for the parents, but for the kids.

When I get to be a father—and I do plan on having children one day (but not one day soon!)—I want to be the kind of father who is just *there* for his children, kind of like my grandfather is always there for me. I want to teach my children right, grow up teaching them the Bible, [to] make sure I leave that imprint and that mark there in my children's hearts so that when outside peer pressures come, they'll already have a solid foundation so that they won't be tempted by outside pressures like so many kids are today. I don't want my children to be confused. I want them to know what is right, and what is wrong.

I just think there's too much confusion in the world today. Young black men need their fathers in their lives. Like me.

as told by David A. Cooley, 15

My wise friend Deacon Dwight Holloway, Sr., of Washington, D.C., is another African American father who offers real-life testimony to the strength of his forefathers and, as is his style, he offers practical solutions for today's black families by looking back on all that was *right* about his own life.

We would do well to listen to the stories of Holloway's past, to the church elder's history. From them, he seems to gain all of his strength and fortitude. Perhaps, if we listen closely to his words, we could gain the same.

"When I was a small boy, the schools went up to the seventh grade," he recalled. "And white people weren't too thrilled to have 'Negro' children going to school at all, if you know what I mean. The white farmers wanted the Negro children to stay home and work the land—the white man's land—so that they wouldn't miss their plowing and tilling their soil," he said in a conspiratorial whisper.

"Well, it was quite a struggle for us to get to school—especially if any of us wanted to go to school past the seventh grade. They made it very hard for us," he added, sounding a little weary.

But then the pride leapt into his voice. He was about to talk about his father.

"I remember—now this was in the mid-1930s—when my father, George Holloway, Sr., went and talked to the white school superintendent in my county about the trouble we were having transporting Negro children to school. Back then, that was a very brave thing to do. But my father was a brave man," he said matter-of-factly.

"The superintendent looked my father right in the face and told him that colored children were not really required to go to school anyway, so he didn't see what all the fuss was about getting help from the county to get one decent bus for the colored children who *did* want to go to school.

"My father was bound and determined to help provide a bus for the students, and he was equally determined to petition the county to see if they could help pay for the bus."

Determined is an understatement, I think.

"So, my father began organizing individuals in the county to help support the idea of getting a bus for those colored students who needed it. He worked hard in an organized way, and he wasn't scared to keep going back to the superintendent with updates on his efforts," Holloway said. "He even met with officials at the Chevrolet company to talk about the possibility of them providing the bus, but they wanted to price it too high. We couldn't have even afforded the interest rate that they were going to charge on the bus, so my father looked at every single possible strategy. One idea was that the county would pay a small amount, then we would have to make up the difference. My father also considered the possibility of raising enough money within the community to pay for the bus completely out of the community's own funds. The most important thing is that my father worked hard, remained determined, and *finally* got the bus he wanted so badly.

"If you go back and check the records even today—check the records of Lunenberg County, Virginia—you'll see that it was my father, George

Holloway, Sr.—who got the ball rolling on providing transportation to the Negro students of the county. Without him, it never would have happened."

And here lies the generational tie.

"That determination seemed to spill right over onto his children, because we were just as determined as he was to seek justice and to have God's will be done, especially on matters concerning race. Because my father was such an activist, in both the community and the church, *I* am an activist even today, in my 'twilight years.' "

He continued.

"This is another thing I learned from the generation that came before me, namely from my father," said Brother Deacon.

"When I was a young child, I remember my father becoming very active in making sure that Negroes in our county got a fair chance to vote, a fair chance at being represented."

He stopped, hesitated.

"Today's generation of fathers and families are torn up, split apart. Fathers aren't in the home the way they used to be when I was coming up. The mothers are mad at the fathers for being gone, and they take it out on their children. And the children, bless their hearts, will never know the joy of living in a home with both parents.

"Like my father, I spend a lot of time in my community and in my church. The other day we had a church dinner for the neighborhood families; you know, just to get the families out, provide them a warm meal, and give them the chance to do something *together*. What broke my heart was that it was mostly young mothers and their babies who showed up. The men who were there didn't seem to be fathers; at least they didn't have any children with them. What these young families need to do to get back on the right track is believe in themselves, bring the Lord into their lives, and love themselves and their children with all their heart. If they loved their children, they'd do everything they could to stay together, to stay married. But that night at the church, I didn't see any 'whole' families together."

I could feel the sadness in his voice.

This wonderful man, well into his eighties, possessed laser-like focus.

He continued. "Today, I am also very active in helping blacks get out and vote and have their voice be heard," Holloway said proudly. "And I know if I hadn't watched how passionate my own father was about justice and opportunity, I might not be as involved as I am now.

"If my father hadn't showed me, I wouldn't have been able to show my own son, and I certainly wouldn't have been as deeply and personally involved in the same issues had it not been for my father. I learned from him, and he, because he was a child of God, helped change the world in his own small way."

He urged me again to do my homework as an author: "Go back to Lunenberg County and see which man made all the difference back then. I guarantee the name you'll find is 'George Holloway, Sr.' Take a trip to Lunenberg and look up its history," he said, almost pleading.

"I'll even pay for your bus ticket."

Deacon Holloway is exactly right. Strong fathers not only breed but actively *teach* strength in their own children. Determined fathers not only make positive change in the lives of others, but if they're faithful fathers, they show their children *exactly how* their personal involvement can make a difference, and encourage that same involvement in their children.

"It's like a cycle," he says simply. "One father starts it, then it passes on to another generation, and another generation, and hopefully it keeps on going so that our wisdom and the lessons we learn will never, ever die."

"Cyclical" is precisely the word, I think, as Mr. Holloway speaks. We owe it to ourselves and to our children to siphon off the best of what our forefathers left for us; to preserve it and pass it along tenderly and with great care, because our history—and the knowledge of the struggles our ancestors faced in order to help get us to where we are today—is what will lead us to solutions.

To some, our ability to be uplifted and spurned to action by the faith of our forefathers is a lost art.

Alex Haley said of the younger generation
of fathers and families:

"They have forgotten the struggle . . .
and they have forgotten the road over which we have come,
and they are not teaching it to their children."

And if we don't teach it to our children, who will? If we have forgotten the struggles of our forefathers, who will help our children remember? How can we pass along to our own progeny the grit and determination of our forefathers if we ourselves allow it to go unnoticed and uncelebrated?

Because we were ripped away from our homeland and brought to America in the shackles and the shadows of slavery, we have an empty, gaping hole into which to gaze when it comes to family continuity.

We cannot let it be our undoing.

That hole I speak of—that "unknowing" of things past that permeates the way we raise our children—only lessens the grandeur and glory of the black fathers of yesterday.

"Of my father, I know nothing.
Slavery had no recognition of fathers, as none of families."
—FREDERICK DOUGLASS,
ABOLITIONIST AND ORATOR

Douglass was right then, and his words still ring true today.

Our family quilts are "coming undone," as are our children and our sense of the proud black father's rightful place in history: a sad and tragic statement, but a true one nonetheless. But one that can be mended.

For us to grow strong, we must reach back and draw from our past.

But to draw from our past means that we have to work hard to keep the memories of our past alive and flourishing. Men like Deacon Holloway do it. Men like Vincent Mathews do it. But it can't be done in isolated pockets. We must reinvigorate the desire within our own hearts to share the strength of our forefathers with our children. Because, at this stage—and I hesitate to utter these pessimistic words but will do so anyway to underscore the urgency—the strength of our past is more alluring than the promise of our future.

To fathers: illuminate the darkness for your children and families.

Pull out photographs, if you have them, of your own fathers and show them to your children. *Explain* to them their family history, at least as much as you know. Connect them to their elders who knew, instinctively, that right was right and wrong was wrong. Let them know that you, too, carry the mantle of paternal pride, a mantle that was passed on to you from those who came before you.

———

Follow these words of educator Booker T. Washington:

"Years ago I resolved that . . . I would leave a record of
which my children would be proud, and which might
encourage them to still higher effort."

———

A record of which our children would be proud. A road map for them to follow when the way grows dark. Let's leave a legacy of pride for our children.

———

Let's read the words in Proverbs 17:6:

"Children's children are the crown of old men;
and the glory of children are their fathers."

———

I, for one, am a lover of crowns—and of glory. Why, you may ask, is it so vitally important that we continue the fight to preserve the precious jewels in our fathers' crowns? Why is this fight necessary for our very survival?

I *know* the answer.

You tell me.

8.

WHEN HURT HAPPENS

VIABLE SOLUTIONS FOR
FAMILIES AND FATHERS IN PAIN

To be sure, there is not a family, black *or* white, in America that has escaped, at one point or another, the ravages of pain. Whether the pain is inflicted by divorce, a sour marriage, a major illness, addiction, recovery, or that complicated thing we call "life," we've *all* winced in the shadows of pain.

But this book is about bright light—not murky shadows. It is about seeking and *finding* the beacons we need when we're being tossed about in stormy seas.

When fathers hurt, they are—traditionally and instinctively—reluctant to express or verbalize their pain in any demonstrative way. Too often, the pain simmers inside their souls like a poisonous stew—quiet, but by no means inert. It grows inside their spirit, eventually seeping out and infecting their families and their daily lives.

Too many of our African American families are suffering invisible pain; far removed from the public eye; blistering behind the closed doors and sealed windows of their homes. Divorce, custody battles, substance abuse, and spousal abuse are the silent demons that we tend to keep hidden from sight.

Pulling these demons out of the darkened closets and into the light of day where, hopefully, they can be exorcised and purged is, for too many black families, considered a stigma; an undesirable and unattainable option. So we suffer these silent demons alone, and in pain. Seeking outside help such as therapy or psychological counseling is considered a sign of weakness and desperation.

The question I put before you is this: When will we finally realize, for those of us who are hurting, that seeking help is actually a sign of strength and empowerment?

I was led by the hand by my Father God directly to several people who devote their lives to helping families in pain, fathers who have lost their way, men and women who are immersed in hopelessness and despair.

Even in the midst of pain, there is joy. Why? Because God makes sure it's *always* there. The trick is to lift it up and find it.

In an effort to gather and share practical, positive solutions for black families who are facing pain and carrying deadly vials of crises deep within their hearts, I sat down with a few African American "experts" who were only too happy to open their doors—and their hearts—to families in trouble.

Their message: *Healing is possible.*

And until we can garner the strength to walk with pride into a therapist's office to seek help, I think I have a solution: if the patient can't make it to the doctor, bring the doctor to the patient!

Which is exactly what I'm about to do.

The Doctor Is In

Deacon Holloway remembers a lot about his father; a lot about how families throughout his entire black community in rural Virginia regarded his father as *the* person to come to when they were in emotional pain.

"When I was a small boy," he says, "I remember how my father was seen as a leader—mostly a spiritual leader—throughout the community. Particularly for matters of the heart and of the spirit, something about my father's advice and guidance always seemed to help ease their pain."

The "original" and authentic version of what we know of today as a marriage counselor and family therapist, I think as he speaks.

"Couples would come to him when they were facing problems in their marriage and ask him for his advice. At that time, divorce and separation weren't really even options, which made it even more important for families to try to seek good help when it came to their children, themselves, and their marriage."

*Of course, the natural follow-up question would be, "What **was** this magical advice, and would he mind sharing it with my readers?" Perhaps, I think to myself, we could modernize it, package it, and offer it to those families facing the conflicts of today.* The deacon heard my question before I even had a chance to ask it.

"Now, I don't know *exactly* what he told people, but I do know that the most important thing they seemed to think was that he *was there* for them in a time of crisis, and that he was a wise man who would listen to their problems without casting judgment or getting in the middle of the mess," he says.

"They'd come and talk to him at home, or invite him to visit after church. And the wonderful thing about it is that he would never turn anybody away. He never thought that any problem was too small. He was really a man who helped try to ease the pain of others."

Not only is the doctor in. But he makes house calls.

Free of charge.

Amen and hallelujah.

Sisters Who Help

I know two healers who know how to help. That they both happen to be my siblings is an added gift. Both have worked hard and dedicated their lives to helping families heal.

One of my sisters speaks of her years as an addiction counselor. She saves lives by extending an outstretched hand to people who are in need; people who have reached or are about to reach the end of their physical and spiritual rope.

"In my practice, I see an alarmingly high number of black men—and black fathers—taking incredible risks with their lives," she says.

"These are men who feel incapable of being good *men*—much less good fathers," she says.

"I hear a lot of 'I just couldn't cope without finding something to take the edge off of my life' or 'The reason I'm strung out on drugs is because I'm a black man in a white man's world.'

"They know that these are the symptoms of something much larger and much more serious, but they feel comfortable using these excuses. It requires professional intervention to help them identify their symptoms, then to act on eradicating them. Many people just can't do this by themselves—nor should they feel they have to.

"Particularly with black fathers who are substance abusers, I tend to prefer group sessions over individual sessions," she explains.

Her following comment mirrors my own views.

"Many black males still aren't comfortable in professional therapy. It's just not a part of our culture. Particularly when their therapist is a female, it sometimes takes too long to get past the stigmas they're still carrying around with them about therapy. With the more severe cases, we just don't have that kind of *time*," she adds with a sense of urgency.

"In group therapy, particularly with men, it's somehow less difficult for clients to open up," she says.

"When we're in one large group, it becomes easier for them to recognize their own vulnerabilities, because they see those same vulnerabilities in someone else sitting right next to them in the same room, and they suddenly realize that they are not alone.

"When men are 'in group,' they often begin playing what I call a 'mirror game'—which is, in my opinion, a very healthy game to play when you're in therapy, particularly if you're having problems looking directly inside yourself. So for the moment, they don't really *need* to look directly at their own flaws or foibles. They can look at and listen to someone else's. They're looking at themselves through the image of someone else! Kind of like holding a mirror to your face and seeing another person's image, a person who has the same problems and pain as you do."

She speaks with ease and confidence.

What she's using is a technique that, in her estimation, helps black men and black fathers take a closer look at themselves by looking more closely at others. Hence, the mirror thing.

"Many of the black males I treat have completely lost *all* hope of ever being good fathers or good men again. It becomes imperative for me, in situations like this, to provide not only the best professional treatment I can, but a measured degree of compassion and understanding as well."

She is a strong believer in the idea that maintaining dignity is essential in recovery and healing.

She knows, from her own personal experience, that seeking professional help and finding personal compassion are two components that will save lives.

Long, long ago, these are the components that saved hers.

She elaborates:

"I wouldn't have survived without others showering me with compassion *early* in my life.

"Daddy and Mother showered me with compassion and support," she says of her earlier days. "So did countless other people whose paths I crossed when I was caught up in my own nightmares. That's when I learned about the inherent value of compassion."

"What I see happening is that African American males would rather stand tall, like skyscrapers, during times of crisis. Many don't realize that it's much more beneficial—and *healing*—to *bend* in the face of pressure, like a sapling in a strong wind. Resilience is key."

The knowledge that resilience is key must come first, however, I think to myself.

"The life pressure my clients face is, in their minds, impossible to deal with on their own, which is the primary reason they resort to temporary, fast-acting 'relaxation' and 'stress reduction' alternatives. Translated: alcohol and drug abuse. The abuse then spins out of control, which causes the rest of their lives to collapse as well. It's a vicious, unforgiving cycle that is extremely difficult to break without professional help.

"I used to have a client who had been struggling with the demands of manhood and fatherhood for quite a long time," she says, remembering.

"It was clear that he loved his children, but he told me—no, he told the others, in group session—that he didn't even know how to change his baby's diapers anymore because he'd been so strung out on drugs. I know it scared him to have to admit this, and it scared several of the other people in the session. It's sometimes the very act of verbalizing this 'rock bottom' of a situation that nudges the person back onto the right track."

How can black fathers get the help they need?

"Sometimes, those who need it most are so deep into their pain that it renders them virtually incapable of caring for themselves, much less for their families. That's why professional therapy is so crucial," she says.

"I don't mean for this to sound hard-hearted or cruel, but if a family is facing a dire crisis where, for instance, the father is a spousal or drug abuser, the most effective intervention oftentimes is to temporarily remove the father from the family. It breaks up the family, but the family has already been emotionally broken and sometimes even destroyed by the nightmare of having to live with an abuser," she says.

She paints a picture that is stark and disturbing.

"A separation has to occur, physically and emotionally, particularly if there are children involved. The separation is often a legal mandate as well; the abuser must get out of the house to avoid the threat of further damage to himself or to his family. A separation also allows time for reflection for every family member. And it allows professionals to move in and begin the task of treatment and rebuilding."

Painful stuff, I think. But necessary steps to take if you're in the middle of it, trying to find your way out.

"Another thing that black families in crisis can benefit from is professional interventions. But, unfortunately, we just don't consider it as an option—either because we're not aware of its benefits or because the entire concept is just too foreign to us, too controversial and countercultural."

Tanya explains professional intervention as "a last-ditch effort to save the family and save the abuser."

But the words "last-ditch" aren't necessarily bad. She mentions again that these rock-bottom efforts are often the ones that truly reach down deep and turn things around—for the better.

Here's how a professional intervention works, she describes:

"An intervention is usually conducted with *every* member of the immediate family, professionally facilitated by a psychiatrist, psychologist, or therapist."

I ask her about the fate of the children who must sustain this familial pain, particularly when it is the father who is experiencing the crisis.

"In most cases, having the children present at an intervention is a *good* thing," she answers. "It helps them understand and validate that their father is sick, and that the entire family loves him enough to try to get help.

"Every member of the family is allowed to speak."

In some cases, black families may *never* have been able to create this kind of controlled environment, where everyone has a chance to be heard without violence, volatility, or threats of retribution.

"I've heard young kids make statements to their fathers during interventions like, 'I *hate* that "medicine" you always take, Daddy, because it makes you act crazy! I *hate* the way you always look out of the window after you take that "medicine" because you're scared someone is going to come and take you away. It scares me, too! I don't want anyone to come into our house and take any of us away!' "

This, she explains, not only offers a wonderful way for the child to vent concerns and frustrations, but it also provides a vital and rare opportunity for the child to be able to communicate directly with his or her father, in a controlled environment, about the crisis that is tearing their family apart.

Such a process benefits everyone—especially those families that aren't accustomed to regular one-on-ones or family sessions with a therapist.

"It gives the older siblings a chance to vent as well," Tanya says.

"An older sister might say something during an intervention like, 'Because you have this problem or that problem, I've had to take on a second job. And I just can't balance two jobs, school, and helping Mom try to take care of the family anymore. It's too much, Dad.' "

Here, the older child has verbalized the burdens she faces (thereby helping to lift them, if only a little), plus she's communicated directly to her father *exactly* how his behavior is affecting—or ruining—her life, without angry accusations and hysterical screaming.

"Then the mother takes a turn," Tanya explains, almost as if it's an intricate, delicate game.

"The mother might say something like, 'I'm not going to lie for you anymore. I won't tell your boss that you're at the doctor when he calls looking for you, and I won't be your enabler anymore. I love you, but I won't let you destroy my family. We *all* want to help you lick this problem, but if you can't—if *we* can't together—then you're no longer welcome in our home because you present too much of a danger to our family.'

"It's not so much an ultimatum as it is a final plea, pure and simple," Tanya says.

"A younger brother might chime in and say to his father, 'What's happened to you, man? You *never* play basketball with me anymore, and you never come up to the school to see my teachers. My friends think there's something wrong with you, and I do, too. You don't even show up at my *games*! And I hate the way you treat Mom when you've been drinking or using. Dad, it's got to stop.'

"All of that is to say that these sessions aren't designed to embarrass the father or to threaten him. What emerges is a natural outgrowth of what the entire family has been through. They're tired, and they want to save the family, but they just don't want to keep trying *if the father isn't going to try for himself*. In many ways, it's the healthiest place to begin.

"Many of these interventions I do free of charge," she says, matter-of-factly, as if in afterthought. "They take up a huge amount of my time—the preparation, the legwork, the follow-up—but I usually perform these without even the *thought* of charging for my services."

Compassion burns brightly in her voice.

"Why? For the hope of renewal without the worry of having to incur a debt. Many of my clients don't have *any* money. They've been in jail. Or they've had to pay bonds. Or pay restitution. Or pay for damages for something they've destroyed. I want to teach not only my clients but their families how to avert crisis and how to deal with it once it's in your face. Usually, attaining that knowledge costs a lot of money—or at least *some*," she says.

A nother angel waits in the wings.

Yet another of my older sisters, Noelle, the psychologist.

She, too, is a wonderful person to turn to when hurt happens. She shares her knowledge happily, generously. Her heart and her smile are as big as the sky.

"When families hurt, every member of the family hurts," she begins.

"In the midst of crisis are when solutions are hardest to find. When you need them *most*, viable solutions are difficult to identify because you've lost your clarity of vision; you've lost your objectivity; and you've momentarily lost your footing. This is when families need to turn away from themselves and seek help," she says.

I love her as much as I love the air I breathe. Everything about her: her smiling, brown face; how she observes life around her; how she always, *always* says "I love you" before we hang up the phone.

"In my practice, I see lots of African American families. Happily, I can say that a small percentage of these families come to me on a periodic basis, for *preventive* counseling, *before* a crisis occurs."

Preventive medicine is always preferable to damage control.

"Black parents—fathers *and* mothers—can slip into patterns of self-destructive behavior so easily that it's frightening," she says. "Particularly after a divorce or separation, when each is hurting and each is searching for ways to ease the pain.

"But the sad part is that when this happens, they are subconsciously making themselves less available for their children, who really need them most during a difficult period of divorce or separation.

"I hope that parents and families who read my words can realize that the *last* thing they want to do during a crisis is slip into behavior that will, unwittingly, distance themselves from their children," she gently warns.

"Recently, a couple came to me for marriage counseling," she says, putting on her no-nonsense "don't ask me any questions about their identity" voice. "The woman was mentally prepared and emotionally ready for a divorce. But what was interesting was that the man recognized that if they *did* divorce, the mother would, more than likely, gain custody of the children."

Noelle continues.

"The father *didn't* want to separate. And the primary reason, I think, was the recognition that he was probably going to be the one to lose the children. He wanted so badly to stay together with his wife. He didn't want to see himself being reduced, suddenly—in his children's eyes—to a monthly support check or weekend visits."

The larger statement she seems to be making wasn't about this particular couple at all, but about how society views—and really devalues, to a frightening extent—black fathers. Although the laws are becoming more progressive each day, the majority of custody battles still end up favoring the mother. What do these laws mean for the father? And how do they impede his ability to "father" his children if he gets to see them only in periodic spurts?

The other larger conclusion I drew from her statement was a much brighter, more optimistic point, which is that *many black fathers cherish their relationship with their children above all else and will make any sacrifices necessary to ensure that they remain together.*

This, of course, is a good thing.

"When all is said and done," she says, "particularly the way the custody laws lean today, even though they're becoming much more progressive, black fathers have to make some tough decisions about how they intend to be involved in their children's lives. Lots of times, in cases of divorce or separation, if both parties are clear-sighted enough to focus on the *children*, it allows fathers the ability to create much more 'pure' and undisturbed relationships with their children—without the contamination and toxicity that comes with bitter divorces, where each party's vision is muddled and cloudy.

"When families are hurting," she says, "the way to stop the pain is to confront it—a hard task to undertake alone. That's when the help of a professional becomes critical."

Harold Washington, former mayor of Chicago,
agreed that confronting pain and finding solutions are
a huge battle, but that it can indeed be accomplished.
Said Washington:

"Most of our problems can be solved. Some of them will take brains, and some of them will take patience, but *all* of them will have to be wrestled with like an alligator in a swamp."

When hurt happens, we are not always equipped to deal with it by ourselves. Especially if the hurt involves children, then we owe it to our kids to swallow our pride, put away our bitterness, and get to someone quickly who can offer objective, professional guidance.

Older teaching younger all the "right moves"

Black families, particularly men and fathers, must remember this. We must work to dismantle the age-old stereotype that visiting a therapist means you're crazy.

It doesn't.

If anything, it means you're more sane.

The ability to sustain and nurture our familial strength and sanity is one we must work at constantly, diligently. Facing this fact—without fear or embarrassment—is what will save our black families.

Here are an African American father and son who are facing life's challenges head-on, with courage and an unabashed, strategic sense of determination to succeed.

Michael A. Tucker, a highly respected playwright, award–winning writer and producer, and a professor at Howard University, is a black father who loves his son beyond measure; who loves him enough to put his professional career on the back burner the moment his son needs him. The epicenter of Mike's universe is his family. His son, Christopher, struggles daily with Asperger syndrome, a high-functioning form of autism. In many subjects, Christopher borders on brilliance. His observations are razor-sharp. His mind leaps ahead and arrives at conclusions long before a question is even put before him. But his autism occasionally nudges him toward mildly socially inappropriate behavior.

Not to worry.

Michael and his wife, Geri, both strong in spirit and buoyed by a faith larger than themselves, are always there to nudge him back to normalcy.

And they work hard to do it right.

"Family therapy is a very important and very real part of out lives," Michael says calmly, matter-of-factly. The therapy is purposefully and comfortably incorporated into their family lives, Michael explains as he glances lovingly at Christopher, who's happily munching on candy and heading upstairs to play PlayStation II with my son.

"We always try to schedule the [therapy] sessions so that Christopher can get home in time enough to do his homework."

Balancing Christopher's brilliance and his autism is an ongoing labor of love. Along with the love, though, come challenges.

"I'll be the first to admit that there is friction between Christopher and me lots of times," Michael says. "But we deal with it. It's a lot of work—like raising *any* child is a lot of work—and we definitely have our difficult moments."

Even though father and son are now in different rooms, the bond between them is palpable, pulsating. My heart smiles with pride.

"Geri and I refuse to let Christopher's autism get in the way of the expectations we have of him," he says, adding, "and our expectations are high."

Amen.

Here is a black father who not only wants the best for his son, but who expects it, receives it, no matter what the circumstances. Here is a man who works hard to provide the resources for his son that will keep him competitive, sharp, and prepared to face the world around him.

"As hard as we work to let Chris know that our expectations of him are high—and always will be—he also knows that we understand the special challenges he faces."

The Tuckers have already given their son more than a head start, more than a leg up. How? By making sure those people who surround their son see him as their equal.

"We work hard to keep Christopher mainstreamed," Mike says, "and he's actually pretty strong in subjects like English and the sciences. Next year, he'll be taking algebra and physics," the father says proudly of his son, "but naturally, there are special nuances that the people who surround him on a regular basis have to recognize."

Christopher is active in sports, loves to read, loves playing the piano, and—it goes without saying—loves his family. Michael works hard to make sure that his son constantly feels that paternal love flowing toward him.

"When I talk about 'nuances,' " he continues, "I'm talking about the

*Michael proudly holding his
one-year-old son, Chris*

nuances that autism creates. But those nuances don't need to be hindrances. What I work hard at is *equalizing* the nuances; and one way to do that is to keep my expectations of him high."

He chooses an example.

"I don't want his teachers giving him a 'break' on his work. He's a bright kid and can pull himself up to the challenge," he says.

The reality of racism is another issue that Michael gently, almost imperceptibly, makes his son aware of—not to scare him, but to better prepare him for the bigotry and hurdles he will undoubtedly be confronted with.

"The bottom line and what I teach Chris is this: that you have to follow the rules. Simple as that. Especially black children. Whatever their class or financial situation, no matter how large or small a house they live in, no matter what their situation is in life, black kids must adhere to a basic level of respect for authority. In order to challenge it, you must first adhere to it."

I listen closely.

"It is the responsibility of black fathers to teach their children the basic rules of society. To teach them respect and adherence. And if the parents don't teach them, the police will—and that, as we all know, can be lethal. So as a father, I take the task of giving my child the tools that he needs to function in society very seriously. The alternative is unacceptable."

I think about the frustration—and, yes, the pain—that Christopher must surely have to face occasionally. At the same time, I say a silent prayer of thanks to God that Chris has a father so committed to uplifting and protecting him that he'll stop at nothing to provide the tools his son will need to face that complicated thing we call life.

On Dickens, Shakespeare, and Beef Jerky

There are so many things I enjoy. I love playing the piano, working with computers, reading, and playing video games. There's lots of things I like to do with my dad, too. We go camping and we read together a lot. I can remember him reading to me even when I was a little kid.

That's probably why I like to read so much now. Because of my dad. He teaches me lots of things. He's usually always there when I need him, too.

I love my family very much, even though my dad and I get into arguments and disagreements a lot. Sometimes he complains about the smallest things I do, but I know he's doing it because he wants me to be a better person. Like, for instance, he loses his temper sometimes when I do the wrong thing or even eat the wrong thing. Recently we were having breakfast and some relatives were over, and I accidentally dropped a muffin on the kitchen floor. He got really angry for no reason at all, which made me say a very bad word because I was angry, too. He was so

Father and son, reading together

Dad offering a higher perspective

shocked that I used that word! But afterward, I apologized to him and he apologized to me. We both realized that we over-reacted. Sometimes that happens with us. Here's something else, too: I really like beef jerky. I don't eat it that often at all— and when I do, I make sure it's the low-sodium, low-fat kind, but my dad doesn't want me eating all of that junk. So we try to compromise and he lets me eat it sometimes. It seems like a little thing, but it's a pretty big thing if you really like beef jerky and your dad doesn't let you eat it.

My mom and dad do lots to help me. I really love them for that because I know it takes a lot of patience.

My Grandma Mavis lives in New York and I love her a lot, too. When the attacks happened on September 11, I was pretty worried about her and was hoping she was okay. Thank goodness she was okay. But I also have a friend at church whose mother was killed during the attacks. I feel so sorry for him.

In a weird way, what happened on September 11 reminds me of one of my favorite books by Charles Dickens called *Great Expectations*. My dad and I have talked a lot about how Dickens's novel relates to September 11, and I have this theory that I think is pretty neat: remember how in *Great Expectations* Miss Havisham blocked herself away from the rest of the world? I compare Miss Havisham to how many of the families who were affected by September 11 are still grieving. It's almost like their grief blocks them out from the rest of the world. Just like Miss Havisham. She boarded up her windows and locked all the doors in her home. She just didn't want to have any part of the outside world, kind of like the families of September 11: their grief is almost blinding them so that they can't even see the rest of the world around them. Remember how poor Miss Havisham died in a fire? So did the victims of September 11. The fire destroyed them. I know it might sound cruel to say—and my dad told me not to say this to my friend whose mother died on that day because it might hurt his feelings—but the families of the victims can't let their own grief kill them. I know it must be really hard—and I've talked with my dad about this a lot—but the families of those people who were killed can't let themselves become like Miss Havisham. No matter how hard it is, they have to move on with their lives. I know it must be really hard for them, and I'm not saying that they should try to forget about it because they shouldn't. They can't. In fact, they should always remember. But they should also know that they'll see their loved ones who were killed in the next life. They'll see them again—not only in the next life, but in every other "next life" that follows after that. That's why I love literature so much. It always relates to the everyday world. Reading with my dad when I was little helped me realize that.

Here's another thing I think about a lot, which also has to do with literature and how I compare it to what happened with the terrorist attacks. And I know how fortunate I am to have a dad who actually enjoys listening to my ideas about these kinds of things: remember in Shakespeare's *Romeo and Juliet*—one of my favorite plays of all time and definitely one of the most tragic—how at the end, when Juliet wakes up to find Romeo dead, she starts crying and wailing? After that, she grabs Romeo's dagger and stabs herself to death. That's another example of how people don't deal all that well with their own grief. Sometimes they let their grief kill them. Sometimes it's just too painful to them that they don't want to live anymore.

These are the kinds of things I think about a lot. I'm really fortunate to have teachers who love to discuss these things with me at school and to have a father and mother who'll talk to me about anything at all.

It really makes things a lot easier for me.

as told by Christopher Tucker, 17

———◆———

Says poet and philosopher Kahlil Gibran of pain:

"Your pain is the breaking of the shell that encloses your understanding. Even as the stone of fruit must break, that its heart may stand in the sun, so must you know pain.

"And could you keep your heart in wonder at the daily miracles of your life, your pain would not seem less wondrous than your joy;

"And you would accept the seasons of your heart, even as you have always accepted the seasons that pass over your fields.

"And you would watch with serenity through the winters of your grief.

"Much of your pain is self-chosen.

"It is the bitter potion by which the physician within you heals your sick self.

"Therefore trust the physician, and drink his remedy in silence and tranquillity: For his hand, though heavy and hard, is guided by the tender hand of the Unseen, and the cup he brings, though it burn your lips, has been fashioned of the clay which the Potter has moistened with His own sacred tears."

———◆———

9.

AN INVITATION TO HEAL

In this book, I have spoken with people who want to heal. I have prayed for healing for myself. Hopefully, my musings will enlighten a mind or two. In my daily life, on the subject of fatherhood and families, I've done quite a bit of praying. Some preaching. Hopefully, never any pedantic lecturing.

But my strongest desire was not to preach or to muse or even to wax sentimental. My strongest desire was to write a book that examined our pain and bitterness without *inciting* it. My strongest desire was to write a book whose words and shared reflections would inform us, uplift us, spur us to action, help us remember, remind us to refuse to forget, and help us learn to heal. God alone guided my pen as I wrote. He directed me to extraordinary people whose shared stories added tenderness and depth to my pages. He's guiding me along this precise path that I'm traveling now.

A healing path. A loving path.

I say all the time that nothing happens without a reason, and that everything that happens in our lives—every breath we take, every word we utter, every creature upon which we lay our eyes—is in some way connected to and guided by God's sure and steady hand, and that, moreover, every one of us is inextricably linked to this universal path—and thereby to each other—whether we like it or not.

I am constantly amazed at how life overflows onto itself, and at the beauty and perfection of God's work. I have surrendered myself to it, which gives me peace in times of pain, calm in the midst of chaos. My own family, like any other, has its share of problems and imbalances. But we know how to communicate, to listen, to heal, and to surrender our problems to the Lord.

And He has accepted them.

How comforting it is to know that He always will.

———◆———

A thought to keep in mind and store away in our souls
as we embark on this chapter on healing,
by the late African American minister Howard Thurman:

"I will yield all the hard places of my heart
to the softening influence of the spirit of God . . .
it will not be easy, not simple perhaps,
but here in the quietness I give up to Him all the lumps, the
unresolved bits of me."

———◆———

The healing words of Howard Thurman bring sweet comfort to my ears, because I myself, as I write these words, suffer from sickness. And in my own current, personal effort to heal this illness that is coursing through my veins, I let go of all the bitterness and give it to God, and wait. Wait until He makes my heart whole again, and my body fully functional.

It is no accident nor is it a random occurrence that I arrive at this chapter on healing—the most crucial, redemptive chapter in this entire book, I believe—being very ill myself. God has led me here, and here I stand; sicker than I've ever been in my life. Weak. Medicated. Distracted by my pain. Determined to place my fingers on my computer keyboard without trembling. I accept both my illness and the timing of its arrival as nothing short of miraculous. It is predetermined. Interconnected. Guided by the hand of God. That He would lead me to this chapter—this "call to healing" that I had been planning to issue for months—at a particular moment when I happen to be at my sickest and weakest point is Divinely inspired.

I want to call—no, *holler*—for healing now because it is not only my own time to wail, but it is time for all of us to heed the call for healing. In a sense, we are—all of us—sick. Weak. Laid low by the pressures of silent demons such as prejudice, hatred, depression, and oppression. We have relinquished our "wholeness" in favor of a fragmented, fabricated community. As a people, we are in dire need of a remedy that can help us recall what we *used* to be; some elixir we can swallow that refocuses our vision and reconstructs our values; some kind of salve that we can apply to the black families that are broken and to the fathers who used to be our kings.

A word to all of the single or divorced mothers who are trying to fill the role of both mother *and* father:

Please stop what you're doing, if only for a moment, and come with me to a healing place.

To the children who've been hurt and who are hurting: put down your pain and take hold of my hand as we walk the slow walk toward recovery and renewal.

To the fathers who feel fragmented from their families and who hold their own children, for whatever reason, in abeyance: leave your guilt where it is—drop it where you are—and come travel a different road with me instead. A road of redemption. A road that holds hope and the promise of reconciliation.

To every mother or father, child or surrogate, mentor or role model who is coming close to losing that last glimmer of hope and wants to simply put their head down on a pillow somewhere and *rest*: come and be still with me. Healing requires rest and stillness.

"Healing time" for father and child is essential

Let us remember, always, that God has His hand in everything, and that everything is in God's hands. He knows what we need before we are even aware of it ourselves—much less able to communicate it to others.

This hope for healing is rooted in something larger than our own experiences. It is rooted in the word of God. When Jesus said to John, "I will not leave you comfortless. I will come to you" (John 14:18), He kept His promise. The comfort came, as did the healing. Why? Because it was a promise made and, of course, a promise kept. Similarly, when Jesus said to His disciples, "Be with me where I am" (John 17:24), He was calling on them to drop their bags, their burdens, and their baggage to simply "be with Him." To be with Him and seek healing and comfort.

Let's drop our baggage at the water's edge and begin a new journey filled with love, laughter, and the indomitable spirit of forgiveness. In the meantime, let's give the pain, the pride, and the poisons we carried around in our hearts for so long *back to God.*

Also, understand this: God doesn't want us to just hand over the ugly and the bad and wait—expectantly and motionlessly—for the good to come by itself.

It doesn't work like that.

He wants us and *expects us* to play an active role in our own recovery. Led by Him, He wants us to lead others. He wants us to bring everyone into this healing fold; first to gain strength, then to begin the walk down the healing path. We cannot afford to stand still, and we certainly can't afford to take a backward step, so our only choice it to forge ahead; forge ahead toward forgiveness, toward redemption, and bathe ourselves in His spirit and in the spirit of forgiveness.

Our choices are few. Either we can learn to love ourselves again and step out into the bright sunshine, or we can retreat behind the shadows and darkened corners of the empty, lonely days that we have not only come to live, but become accustomed to living. There is no middle ground. Healing does not lend itself to middle ground.

Nor does love.

EPILOGUE

There is an ancient African symbol called *sankofa* that represents the theory that our future is inextricably linked to our past, and vice versa. The mythical sankofa bird was able to fly forward while looking backward. The concept of sankofa, therefore, more closely connects us with each other and helps us make more collective sense of what our future holds, as we more closely examine our past.

Sankofa is a notion both tender and indispensable.

If we hold it very, very close to our hearts, similar in manner to how a father would hold his fragile, newborn infant, sankofa will anchor us. It will allow us—even encourage us—to swoop and soar and scratch the sky, all the while having our feet firmly planted on rich, solid soil; the very soil our ancestors tilled until their spirits were badly bent, but never broken.

Sankofa must be inhaled, as deeply as you'd inhale that thick, comforting scent of the lilac tree in your grandfather's backyard—with your eyes closed and your face turned upward toward the sun and the sky. It cannot be reduced to an empty cliché or a politically correct buzzword. In order to work, it must be absorbed. Acted upon. Purposefully, passionately taught, celebrated, and reaffirmed in the hearts of all of us who are African American and interested in assuring a solid future for our race.

As I've said in earlier chapters, it is hard to heal, particularly for African American men who are fathers. Actively swimming a stroke that allows black men to keep their own heads above water is effort enough. As an adolescent, I remember well visiting my maternal grandfather, watching him and my father gently swaying on his front porch glider, smiling quietly and talking in low voices. Mostly it was my grandfather who spoke, but I could tell my father was listening carefully, "with both ears":

"Marriage, having and raising children, teaching them that right is right and wrong is wrong—it's all more than a notion," my granddad would say, holding his pipe in his right hand and inhaling deeply. Many elders I know and love have said the same thing, and they are, of course, exactly right: it is more than a notion. It is hard, purposeful work by anyone's definition.

Black fathers: take heed in the words and lessons of your elders. Work to be good, solid fathers in the same way the elders did. Celebrate what they did right. Avoid, at all costs, those things they did wrong. Stretch toward your family like you've never stretched before. Place yourselves back on the mantel, with the active assistance from us, from those who love you and want to be loved back. Like a Hatha yoga stretch, there is always just a little more room for elongation, no matter how far advanced you may be as a yoga practitioner; just *a few inches more* and something will come into contact with something else that has never been touched before.

Seek help in healing; from professionals, from those you love or used to love, from our Father above. But know that this will be, for the most part, an internal battle. A battle waged against pride. Against love lost. Against pain and humiliation.

◆———

Jesse Owens once said something so elegant in its simplicity
that it deserves to stand alone:

"The battles that count aren't the ones for gold metals.
The struggles within yourself—
the invisible, inevitable battles inside all of us—
that's where it's at."

As you turn inward, flip through the chapters of this book once more. Stand where you are and be conscious. Be strengthened and propelled by the absolute knowledge that there is not one father among you, rich or poor, adoptive or blood-related, weak or strong, who can positively assert that he knows everything there is to know about healing and redemption. It comes from someplace larger than yourselves. It comes from our Father above, and from the fathers who came before us.

It wasn't until a close friend of mine took the time to draw a verbal picture of this concept of the sankofa that I realized such a symbol even existed. In bold, beautiful brush strokes, she described to me the significance of this "can't-look-forward-without-first-looking-backward" notion that links our past to our future.

Here's what it looks like:

Doesn't it look familiar, now that you've seen it?

Haven't you seen this African symbol in its modern form? Perhaps, as you've passed an elaborate, gated courtyard, intricately and deliberately soldered into the gate's fancy grillwork?

It is a symbol virtually all of us have seen but few have recognized or appreciated for its historical significance. Often carved into modern-day sculpture, blended onto a contemporary canvas, or woven into family quilts, it exists as a constant reminder from our ancestors that we are inextricably linked to our past. And if our future is to make sense to any of us in a collective sense—if it is to bear the weight of meaning, continuity, and sustainability—it must, by definition, include the history of our people.

———◆———

Author Wil Haygood stretches deeply into a
mental yoga-like position with these words,
which also deserve to stand alone:

"I know of the cold statistics out there.
And yet, the mountain of father-son literature
does not haunt me. I've known good black men."

———◆———

Let's not, in Haygood's words, "haunt" ourselves with the cruel, cold facts about black fathers, although we all know they exist and they must be dealt with.

Rather than be haunted, let us heal.

The future of our families depends on it.

PHOTO CREDITS

Pages 24, 31, 34, 42, 79, 89, 122, 149: courtesy of the author; pages 41, 48, 80, 81, 134, 145, 154, 175, 186: Jason Miccolo Johnson; pages 101–104: Melissa Dabney; page 155: Valerie Cooley-Elliott; pages 178–180: Michael and Geri Tucker.